ENERGY VAMPIRE SLAYING: 101

How to combat and defeat toxic attitudes and negative behavior in your office,
your home, and yourself

By Dan O'Connor

Designed by Jean Schmith and Dan O'Connor

ISBN-13: 978-1463535087
ISBN-10: 1463535082

For more infromation about the author, and for the free resrources that go along with this book, visit http://www.powerdiversity.com

INDEX

ALSO INCLUDED:

Quick-Reference Cards

Daily Principle Cards

IN THE BACK OF THIS BOOK!

Introduction

You may think you found this program, but you didn't--it found you, and it was no accident. You have been *called*. Don't read one more word or listen to one more second of this program until you are without distraction, and can focus for 30 minutes on your first lesson. You have been called to cast out darkness; you have been called to rid your office of negativity; you have been called to make your home and your life an example of what greatness looks like.

You have been called to become a Slayer.

You *must* be ready or you wouldn't have found this program. The time has come for you to change your office, your home, and your world **before it changes you**.

First, let me tell you who I am. I'm Dan O'Connor, The Energy Vampire Slayer, and I'll be your instructor for this course. I am ***The*** Energy Vampire Slayer. I am on a mission. I have been a motivational speaker and professional communication trainer for over 15 years, and have been slaying Energy Vampires my entire life. I have helped thousands of people and organizations transform their environment through effective communication training. The testimonials of how lives and companies have changed are countless. I help people develop their communication and dealing-with-difficult-people skills every day. I am in the business of transformation, and this is your invitation to join me.

Now it's your turn.

Where are the Energy Vampires (or EVs) in your life? Are you dealing with difficult people at work? Negativity at home? How are you managing your own negativity? Do some people seem to be sucking the life and joy right out of you? What are you doing about it? How are *you* contributing to negativity in the workplace? Do you bring joy into your home and romantic relationships, or do you grab the negativity that's thrown at you, and bring it right into the most important relationships in your life? Basically, are you spreading light or darkness? I'll guarantee you that you're doing one of these things, because there is no neutrality in the universe. You are either bringing people up or bringing them down, *and they're doing the same to you.* Either they are transforming you—in one way or another—or you are transforming them.

Energy Vampires are ***everywhere***. They're in your office, they're in your home, and they're in you. EVs are dangerous, and you need to combat and defeat them, or in other words, slay the Energy Vampires *in* you and *around* you. It's time to discover and release your inner Slayer.

Before we go any further, I must reveal the first **Slayer Principle**:

Energy Vampire Slaying is about *you*.

Stop and take a breath as you say, "This is about me."

Now do it again.

One more time.

AAAAAAhhhhhhh...

It's not about your co-worker who is a back-stabber; it's not about your mother-in-law who is a but-insky; it's not about your out-of-control teen. It's about you. How they behave is about them, how they talk is about them, what they do is about them. How you respond is about you. How you behave is about you. How you talk is about you. **What you do is about you**.

To become a Slayer yourself you must first realize that it's not about actually vaporizing other people--it's about YOU. Even if you were able to eliminate the Energy Vampire that's plaguing you, it is a universal law that there would just be another one to take its place until you change what *you're* doing.

The first question we will address is not what you will DO, but rather who you will *BE*.

This is lesson one, and the lesson which is the most difficult for most *Slayers in-training*. Some never graduate to lesson two. If you can, however, first acknowledge that it's *not* about them, but about *you*, and you will be on your way to becoming a great Slayer. This journey is not an easy one, but if it were easy, everyone would do this, *right*?

In this series, I will teach you verbal communication skills you can use when dealing with difficult co-workers, Gossips, Time-Suckers, and out-of-control customers, so you can put a stop to their behavior (at least when they're around you). You *really can* teach people how to treat you! You'll learn step-by-step effective communication strategies that will help you stand your ground and communicate confidently with difficult people and EVs without *becoming a difficult person yourself.* And if you follow this training program, **you'll begin to see results immediately**.

Each daily lesson will consist of three parts—theory, tactics, and tools. Theory is the concept, tactics help you implement the concept, and tools help you develop and practice your tactics until you master them. You'll see what I mean as we go along.

You should study and practice only one lesson per day. There may be days where you'll get so excited, you'll want to do two or more lessons in the same day, but becoming a Slayer takes time and discipline, and even if you *do* read future lessons, **beware of moving too quickly**. These lessons are organized as they are for a reason, and it takes at least one day of practice per-lesson to achieve maximum results. One week might be even better….

Before you begin your journey, I must give you this warning: The path to becoming an Energy Vampire Slayer is difficult because it is self-revealing. You will see things differently from how you saw them before. You will begin to recognize patterns in yourself that have not served you, and you will be confronted with stronger Energy Vampires than you ever imagined existed. However, if you are disciplined, determined, and committed to the process, the rewards you will reap will be beyond your wildest expectations.

Now if you're ready...let's begin.

Take a deep breath.

Then turn to chapter one.

Chapter 1: Deciding who you are before others decide it for you

FIRST, THE THEORY:

As I mentioned in the introduction, the first question we must ask ourselves when dealing with difficult people, or with any communication training, is not simply what do I do when yadda-yadda-yadda...or what do I say when blah-blah-blah...or what do I tell so-and-so when...

"WHAT DO I DO?" IS *NOT* THE QUESTION!

The first **Slayer Principle** you should refer to when dealing with negativity in the workplace, at home, or in yourself, is this--the question you should be asking yourself is NEVER, *"What do I do?"* The question, rather, is, and should always be:

Who am I going to be?

Repeat this **Slayer Principle** after me:

"In this moment I have a choice.

In this moment I can choose to conform.
or
In this moment I can choose to transform"

This is something I'd like you to say silently to yourself throughout the next 24 hours when you are confronted with negativity at work, at home, and in yourself, or whenever you deal with difficult people. This should be your mantra:

"In this moment I have a choice.

In this moment I can choose to conform.
or
In this moment I can choose to transform"

There is a moment between event and response; a sliver in time between *what is happening* and *how you will respond* to what is happening. Most of us fly right through this sliver in time without thinking, and react to people and situations by saying the first thing that comes into our brains. In other words, we *react*. However, the savvy communicator--the powerful person--the *Slayer*, recognizes this moment in time, and pauses to reflect before responding. This is the difference between *reacting* and *responding*.

One of the first steps in releasing your inner Slayer is: **Get out of the *reaction* mode and into the *response* mode.**

Now, to implement this theory, you need a **tactic, or a strategy to help you behave differently from the way you have behaved in the past**. The way you have responded in the past has evidently not served you as you had hoped, or we wouldn't be together now.

This is why you create and use a **Personal Compass**. A Personal Compass is what you use as your guide when the world around you starts to distract you from the truth of who you are—namely a positive influence in the world. You are here to reflect your maker/your source. **You are here to show the world what greatness *looks like*.**

At times, however, your actions don't necessarily reflect that truth, *wouldn't you agree*?

At times, we get so distracted by mortal illusions, we begin to become Energy Vampires ourselves--that is, we begin to behave as difficult people do. We all do it. You do it; I do it. At times, I let these Energy Vampires around me actually trick me into thinking **I** am an Energy Vampire (or EV) *myself!* That's the EV's job--to convert you--to create other EVs,--to prey on and *suck the life out of* as many people as they can. Conversion is the name of their game...they want to covert us, and sometimes I—like you--fall prey. Sometimes I say and do things that are not reflective of the best of me, but rather are more reflective of the EV I'm up against!

As a human being, if an EV says something nasty to me, my reaction is to say something nasty right back. You insult me, I want to insult you right back. Your ego speaks to me; my ego wants to speak back to you. That's common. The way of the Slayer, however, the way of the savvy communicator, the way of the powerful peaceful warrior, is *uncommon*.

NOW, THE TACTIC:

The Slayer pauses during this moment between event and response, *this sliver in time*, and reflects upon his or her Personal Compass. This is when the magic occurs.

I will now tell you the secret to making your Personal Compass:
You simply fill in the following blanks!

How would you complete the following sentences?

I am _____.

I'm here to _____.

I want _____.

I will _____.

Now, I don't mean to say that you'd fill in the blanks by simply saying, "Well, I am Dan, I'm here to become a Slayer, I want money, and I will slash my coworkers tires in the parking lot if they say one more thing to me. That's not what I mean.

We all go crazy during emotionally charged situations, and EVs tend to push our buttons and make us emotional. Thousands of years of evolution have trained our brains to release chemicals that make us crazy (out of our right mind) when people attack us physically, verbally, or emotionally. It is common to get emotional and go crazy, and say crazy things that we later regret. That's just common human nature. What is *uncommon* is being able to resist our animal instinct, and respond in a savvy, confident, powerful manner. What is *uncommon* is being able to say to yourself:

- "I know who I am
- I know why I'm here
- I know what I want, and
- I know how to get it"

When times get tough.

Completing these sentences may take some time, but it's worth it. I'll walk you through the first step in this lesson.

Step 1:

Decide who you are. Flip to your workbook, and go to page 1. Make a list of the 10 most important roles you play in your life. Each role is just a one-word noun. For example, I, Dan O'Connor, am a son, a brother, an uncle, a partner, a teacher, a student, a citizen, a friend, a speaker, and a professional. Make a list of the top ten things that you are. You can always make it longer, but start out with 10. If you can only think of five, then five. This list will grow.

Then:

Take your list, and add adjectives to it. For example, I am a kind, honorable, loving son. I am a patient, compassionate teacher; I am a responsible, up-standing citizen. This list will also grow.

These statements, or positive affirmations if you will, should not change when your environment changes. For example, if I am a respectful, honorable, generous, responsible citizen, I am that way when everybody is watching, and when no one is watching. I remain the same, even when the people around me aren't behaving respectfully or honorably. I remain the same at the grocery store as well as the office, and with customer service personnel as well as store owners. We all know people who are very Christian at church, and then come to work and behave as though they are wicked devil-worshipers who are bound and determined to drag their entire office down into the fiery pit of hell.
That is an example of what NOT to do.

Forgive them--they just don't have a Personal Compass--they have never been through Slayer training--they know not what you now know, which is: **How you behave anywhere, is how you behave everywhere. How you treat anyone is how you will treat everyone. How you do anything is how you do everything. You are either a Slayer all the time, or none of the time.** THAT IS THE GOAL—TO BE A Slayer TOTALLY, COMPLETELY, IN ALL ASPECTS OF YOUR LIFE.

With that said, I have to make a confession: _I don't always hit the mark every time_. I don't always get it right. In fact, most of the time I _don't_ get it right. But with the right tools I can get it right one more time today than I did yesterday, and if I got it right once out of a hundred times today, with the right tools, I can, and you can, get it right twice out of a hundred times tomorrow. Your powers will compound and grow quickly. You'll be amazed.

It is up to YOU to decide who you are regardless of the person you're talking to. Remember, how **they** treat **you** is about **THEM**. How **you react** to them is about **YOU**. Many people ask me how to _win_ a battle with an EV, but they don't really know _what that means_. Many people are still in a win-lose mentality. For someone to win, someone else must lose. That is a total illusion and delusion. **This is a win-win universe**, and when dealing with difficult people, or EVs, remember that the win for you is that you remain strong and steady, and honor who the best of you is. The win for you is that you will not give in to your animalistic, barbaric, savagery, and say or do things that are not reflective of who the best of you really is. The win for you is that you learn how to respond, rather than react to difficult people. The win for them is that they get to see what a powerful person, a savvy communicator, a real Slayer *looks like*. That's a pretty powerful thing.

Once you have your, "I am" statements completed, you will refer to them during challenging situations *before* you respond. What you will find is that you'll be at home talking with your spouse, or your child, or you'll be at work talking to a coworker, and they will say or do something to push your buttons, and you'll want to do something along the lines of what you've always done and *react*.

But you won't.

You'll remember, and think to yourself, "Hey--I feel like saying to this person, "Don't be such a jerk..." or "How many times do I have to tell you..." or, "Yeah, we'll you're a big ..." and instead of saying what you've always said, you'll remember, "*When I was sane and sober, before I let the delusion in front of me drug me and trick me into thinking that I myself am a difficult person, I wrote down that I am a loving wife, a supportive mother, a loyal coworker--and what I want to say right now **is not** what a loving wife, a supportive mother, or a loyal coworker would say,*" and you'll choose a different path. You'll speak differently— from your higher self.

And you'll be grateful that you took the time to begin developing your Personal Compass.

And you'll have a ***turning point.***

You'll have that turning point because you'll respond differently from how you have responded in the past. You'll respond in a way that is more reflective of the greatness that is in you. You'll respond in a way that is more genuine, more enlightened, and more powerful. You will respond the way a *Slayer* responds.

YOu will respond this way because you will be distinguishing ***fact*** from ***truth***.

This concept will be discussed more in depth in future lessons, but for now, suffice it to say that facts are what aggravate you, facts can be negative, facts draw you away from your source. Truth, however, will, *as they say*, set you free. Truth makes you feel peaceful, truth brings you happiness, truth is always positive, always real and unchanging. Truth brings you closer to your source.

So your assignment for today is to complete step one of creating your Personal Compass—i.e. to develop "I am" statements such as, "I am a loving, patient, nurturing mother," or, "I am a calm, fair, polished professional."

Then, as you go through the next 24 hours, when you start to notice negativity creeping into your world, before you respond to it, remember who you are, and later, *what to do* will come more naturally, **and will be more powerful**.

NOW FOR THE TOOL:

Stop by my website, www.powerdiversity.com, enter the library, and go to our "customer resources" section. There you will find quick-reference flash-cards for Energy Vampire Slaying:101 . Print out these flash-cards (if you have not already printed them out). I suggest printing them out on postcard paper you can easily find at any office supply store. I recommend this, because I have designed these cards to be printed on this paper, which is similar to card-stock, and the paper is perforated perfectly for you to then divide it into cards which fit in your pocket— cards that you will carry with you throughout your day. For day one of your training, print out page one of the Energy Vampire Slaying flash cards, and you'll see that one of the cards reads "Personal Compass." Print this card, and keep it visible all day. Put it up around your workspace, or around your house (or both)— wherever you tend to spend the most time. When you leave, it fits right in your pocket...put it there, and take it out and look at it every time you leave or arrive at any location. Look at it and reflect on it at least 10 times during day one. You can either fill in the blanks or just leave it as is, and it will help remind you of your lesson of the day.

Don't go to day 2 until you have reflected on your "I am" statements
at least 10 times during a 24 hour period.

This will be your first Energy Vampire Slaying lesson. All other lessons rely on you mastering this first step. This lesson, although simple, is not easy. It's probably something you've never done before. That's good. Remember, if you always do what you have always done, you will always get what you have always gotten. If you think the same way today as you thought yesterday, you will get the same results as you got yesterday. If you speak to people the same way you spoke to them yesterday, you will have the same experience you had yesterday. Were you perfect yesterday?

This has been your lesson for today.

Once you've completed this lesson, you can proceed to lesson two. If you need any help, please feel free to visit our website at www.powerdiversity.com where you'll find tons of useful tools—all free-- for dealing with negativity in the workplace, including videos, audios, links, blogs, advice columns, and many others.

Good luck. Until our next lesson.

Homework:

- For the next 24 hours, when you are confronted with a negative person or a negative environment, repeat the **Slayer Principle**, "In this moment I have a choice. In this moment I can choose to *conform*, or in this moment I can choose to *transform*" silently to yourself 3 times or more.
- Finish your "I am" statements on pages 1 and 2 of the ENERGY VAMPIRE SLAYING: 101 WORKBOOK.
- Print out the quick-reference flash-cards that accompany this program in the customer resources section in The Library at www.powerdiversity.com and keep the "Personal Compass" quick-reference flash-card in your pocket. Refer to it at least 10 times throughout the day before your next lesson.

For the resources that go with this and other chapters, including audio recordings and quick-reference cards, go to http://powerdiversity.com/the-library

Chapter 2: Deciding why you're here before others decide it for you

Welcome back, Potential Slayer. By now you should have completed your, "I am" statements from lesson 1, and printed out the Energy Vampire Slaying: 101 Workbook. If you haven't, or if you came across this lesson without having read or listened to lesson 1, go back and complete the first lesson of this program. Without it, you can go no further.

FIRST, THE THEORY:

It's now time for you to decide **why you're here**. I don't mean why you're here reading this book, or there at your office. I mean, why are you here on the *planet*? What's your *purpose*? What gifts do you have that you are meant to share? What brings you joy? What aligns you most with your source?

Making your, "I'm here to ___" statements is step two in making a Personal Compass.

For example, "I'm here to learn," or, "I'm here to teach," or, "I'm here to love and be loved." These "I'm here to ___," statements, just like the, "I am ___" statements will not change if you're at work or if you're at home. They won't change if you're talking to your coworker or if you're talking to your best friend. Whatever you're here to do, you're here to do it **all** of the time. You're here to do it with **everyone**. You're here to do it *even when you think there's nothing in it for you*.

What we tend to do, however, is let *others* dictate to us why we're here.

For example, let's say you're at work, and a co-worker puts you down in front of other people. Your natural reaction is to put them down right back, right? That's what most of us *want* to do. But is that what you're *here* to do? Make people feel bad about themselves? I don't think so. Or suppose your spouse or child is getting on your nerves by lying on the couch instead of helping you with the housework. Your natural reaction might be to say something such as, "Would it **kill** you to get off the couch and help me *for once*?" But is that what you're here to do? Nag people and say things that are insulting or confrontational? I don't think so. Or you might be in the situation where your boss is delivering your performance review (*the number one de-moralizing activity that goes on in most organizations, by the way*) and while you're being told how many mistakes you made, your reaction might be a defensive one; you might just want to tell your boss that you are **the only one** who really works in your office.

But is that really what you're here to do? Prove your worth to other people? I don't think so.

Normally our thought patterns and verbal patterns are a result of, or reaction to, what other people say or do, rather than a reflection of who we are and what we're here to do. Don't fall into that trap.

You are meant for more.

You are not here to **react** to others.

You are here to *express your greatness*.

Only **you** can decide what that is, and how you'll express it.

NOW, THE TACTIC:

That's what your "I'm here to ___" statements help you do. They help you remind your ***future self*** why you're here, when mortal illusions start to distract you from your truth. You create these affirmations when you're sane and sober, so that when life makes you crazy and chemically unbalanced, you will have something to remind you of the truth of who you are and why you're here.

For example, you might affirm "I am here to teach," and/or "I am here to learn," or "I am here to unite and bring joy to my family." I have things such as, "I am here to transform the lives of the people I meet," and "I am here to cast out darkness with the light that's inside me," and "I'm here to enjoy myself."

That last one is a big deal with me--"I'm here to enjoy myself." Years ago I realized that I wasn't enjoying my life as much as I could, and I realized that I was *choosing* not to do so. Now I get it--I can choose to enjoy myself even as I'm waiting in the security line at the airport, or even when I'm stuck in a traffic jam, or even when I'm working late on a Friday night. I can choose to enjoy myself, or I can choose to be miserable—which is the choice people make too often.

Now, I realize that there are things that happen in life that aren't enjoyable. For example, try as I may, I doubt I'll really enjoy myself during my next root canal. I mean, I suppose it depends on the gas they give me, but I really doubt I'll be humming zippidee-do-dah any time during the procedure. The vast majority of the time, however, my thought patterns are directly affecting my mood, and the attitude with which I do things. This is why I memorized this line, and say it not just silently, but out loud many times throughout the day:

16

**I am here to enjoy myself, and
how I do anything is how I do everything.**

Remember that.

Here it is again:

**I am here to enjoy myself, and
how I do anything is how I do everything.**

It's amazing that when I started using my Personal Compass and "I'm here to ___" statements, my life totally changed. Just today, for example, I went to Home Depot in Guadalajara, Mexico. (If you have never been to a store such as Home Depot in an emerging country, you really should go. It would give you a great appreciation of how great US customer service *really* is.) As I was walking in the door, I felt a sick feeling in my stomach because I believed that it would be an ordeal, as it normally is, to get what I needed. I am remodeling my kitchen at the moment, and every time I go to Home Depot for the next step in the remodeling process (today's step was making the final payment and scheduling the installation of the cabinets) it takes hours. Literally.

So I was walking in the door fully anticipating (and probably manifesting) a total and complete drag. Half-way through the parking lot I realized what I was doing, and stopped, and said to myself, "Hey, I'm here to enjoy myself," and my brain started trying to figure out ways to do so. I could literally *feel* the new connections and circuits being formed. Just then, I remembered that I had my MP3 player in the car, and I had just downloaded the book, "The Five Love Languages," and I went back and got the player.

I still sat in a chair for over an hour and a half while people ran around like headless chickens, and occasionally they would stop to ask me the same questions over and over again. But as I sat there waiting, I laughed and I learned and I enjoyed myself. Then as I was leaving, I remember thinking to myself, "Wow! That was enjoyable!"

Why was it enjoyable? Because I was there to enjoy myself. But that's me.

What are you here to do?

You know how sometimes at work, you're tempted to speak from your ego and **really let someone have it**, or teach them a lesson that you think they need to

17

learn and that you are uniquely equipped to give them? Maybe they do need to learn a lesson, but the truth is that it is not up to you to teach it to them. It's up to them to learn it. The best we can do is be an example. (Of course, our children are a whole different story.)

Or you know how sometimes you're at home, or on a date, and you're about to say something hurtful out of anger? I don't know why you're here, but I do know you aren't here to be a jerk, or to be a total downer, or to hurt people. You aren't here to be egotistical, or the boss of the world, and you aren't here to be the nastiest, most unenlightened communicator in the hallway at work.

It just appears that way sometimes, doesn't it?

Slayer Principle:

Life is mostly an illusion.

I spent way too much of my life letting the people and circumstances around me dictate my behavior. Those days are gone, and soon they'll be gone for you too. It just takes practice. Remember, if it were easy to be a Slayer, everyone would do it. If it were easy to be who you were meant to be, everyone would be who she or he was meant to be, and if it were easy to be a better person than you were yesterday, there would be no Energy Vampires. But it's not easy, and there are Energy Vampires.

This lesson helps reinforce what we discussed in lesson one--how what others choose to be is about them, and who you choose to be is about you. What others choose to do is about them, and **what you choose to do is about *you*.**
It's all about you.

It always has been. That's the truth. But you've been sucked in to the negativity, right? We all have--that's a fact.

Never let *facts* get in the way of the *truth*.

I'm sitting still in front of my computer writing this right now. That's a **fact**. It's a **fact** that I'm sitting in my house in Guadalajara, Mexico. You're probably sitting still while you're reading this, or listening to this. That's a **fact**. The truth, however, is that we are both hurtling through the universe at thousands of miles per hour. That's the **truth**. It just doesn't feel that way in this moment.

We get distracted by mortal illusions.

Look at this piece of paper, or the instrument you're using to listen to this book. It's solid, right? That's a fact. The truth, however, is that it's mostly empty space made up of little molecules moving so quickly, that they give the *illusion* that it's a solid object, and it's an illusion that these things around us are different things...the **truth** is that it's all the same stuff...***we're all*** the same stuff. That's the **truth**. We are killing each other all over the world every day using new, creative methods of death and torture. That's a **fact**. We're all brothers and sisters. That's the **truth**. Things and people just look a little different, just like every wave in the ocean looks a little different from the one next to it, but each wave is part of the same ocean, isn't it? That's the truth. Sometimes we are so busy identifying ourselves as unique waves that we forget the truth that we are all part of the same ocean.

My mother is a difficult person. **That's a fact**. She looks like Judge Judy (who, by the way, I believe is drop-dead gorgeous—in case my mother has access to this book); that's a **fact**. She's also a *Sniper*, that's a **fact**. She went to that mother school—the one where mothers go to learn how to push their children's buttons *with just one word*, and she is a *master* at that skill. It was the same school that *her* mother attended. Those are all **facts**. She gets on my nerves sometimes. That's a **fact**, and when she does, I want to say and do things sometimes that don't *really* reflect what I wrote in my Personal Compass.

That's why in my Personal Compass I have things such as, "I am an honorable son," and "I am here to love and learn." That's the ***truth***. Sometimes, however, the things that pop into my brain that I'd like to say to my mother don't really *reflect* that truth. The **truth** is that I'm so grateful to have a mother. **Period**. I'm grateful to have *her* as my mother. I'm grateful to have a supportive mother. That's the **truth**. I am blessed to have that sacred relationship in my life. **Truth**. And some day I'll wish that the phone could ring just one more time with her on the other end of the line, annoying me. And it won't ring. And I'll be sad. That what she tells me, anyway--and I'm afraid it's going to be—the **truth.**

That's the ***truth***.

But boy, my mother can distract me from that truth with one word. You know what I mean? One off-handed comment. One criticism—laced with humor that's not funny. However, armed with my compass, I remember the truth, I see the truth, and I become who I am—a loving, faithful son whose job does not include laying his mother low. (Doesn't life do a good enough job of laying people low, without our adding to it?)

Don't let *facts* distract you from *truth*. Remember, truth ALWAYS makes you feel good, makes you feel at peace, and brings you closer to your source. Facts make you feel uneasy, or angry, or frustrated, and draw you away from your source.

Having a Slayer tool such as a Personal Compass will help you remember who you are and *why you're here* when the world starts to distract you from your truth.

NOW FOR THE TOOL:

It's now time to take out your workbook again. Fill in the page and the flash-card for your, "I'm here to ___" statements, which will eventually be a part of your Personal Compass.

This might be difficult for you, and it shouldn't be done all at once. Do as much as you can right now, but then, during the next 24 hours, when you find yourself feeling uneasy, frustrated, angry, or anything but good, decide what you'd like be doing. For example, "I'm here to give and receive great love." Watch how your behavior will change if you stop during that sliver in time between event and response and refer to your Personal Compass, and your, "I'm here to ___" statements.

When you think of your, "I'm here to ___" statements, write them down. You can't really have enough, but gather at least ten of them.

Do not proceed to lesson three until you have at least ten "I am ___" statements, and ten "I'm here to ___" statements. If it takes more than 24 hours, so be it. How long it takes you is not as important as doing it the right way, and fully completing each lesson.

Sometimes the journey to becoming a Slayer is a long one, but if you are diligent, your powers will increase and you will become a Slayer/energy transformer/light worker, or whatever you wish to call it.

And while you go through the next 24 hours remember this

Slayer Principle:

You are either *conforming* to your environment, or you are *transforming* your environment. There is no neutrality in the universe.

Any object placed in any environment is either reflecting that environment, becoming like that environment, and taking on characteristics of that environment, or that environment is reflecting that object, becoming like that object, and taking on characteristics of that object. This is a law. It happens, in a petri dish, it happens in our office, and it happens in our home. Our environment has a LOT of power! The good news is, you have more. Use it, and use it wisely.

This has been your lesson for today.

Once you've completed this lesson, you can proceed to lesson three. If you need any help, please feel free to visit our website at www.powerdiversity.com where you'll find tons of useful tools for dealing with negativity in the workplace, including videos, audios, links, blogs, advice columns, and many other free resources.

Good luck. Until our next lesson.

Homework:

- For the next 24 hours, when you are confronted with a negative person or a negative environment, repeat the **Slayer Principle**, "Never let *facts* get in the way of the *truth*" silently to yourself 3 times or more. Look for some truth that brings you closer to your source. This will help you differentiate facts from truth more easily.
- Review your answers from pages 1 and 2 of the ENERGY VAMPIRE SLAYING: 101 WORKBOOK.
- Finish your "I'm here to..." statements on page 3 of the ENERGY VAMPIRE SLAYING: 101 WORKBOOK.
- Print out and select one of the *Slayer Principles* cards that accompany this program, and carry it around with you for 24 hours. Pull it out and read it out loud at it at least 5 times throughout the day.

For the resources that go with this and other chapters, including audio recordings and quick-reference cards, go to http://powerdiversity.com/the-library

Chapter 3: Deciding what you want so you can get it now

You made it thorough our first two lessons, Potential Slayer! By now you should know who you are and why you're here. But now you have to accomplish a task so daunting, most people go through their entire lives without accomplishing it.

Remember that you can take as much time as you need to complete each lesson, but you must complete this before moving to lesson 4.

I have faith that you, as a chosen one, will be diligent until you accomplish this task. So take a deep breath and get ready.

Are you ready?

Today's lesson is:
You have to figure out what you want and how you're going to get it.

Don't worry, I'll help you.

Remember that being a Slayer starts with strengthening the *self*. So many Potential Slayers (or Potentials, as I might refer to them) come to me wanting to start slaying day one, but remember--you have to always start with *you*. One of the mantras of a real Slayer is, "**It's all about me**." If you go out into the world to start slaying before deciding who you are, why you're here, what you want, and how you're going to get it, you will be doomed.

That's right—**DOOMED**—to failure.

By the time you finish lesson 3, you will be able to do what very few people can— namely, articulate who you are, why you're here, what you want, and how you will get it. Lessons 1 and 2 covered who you are and why you're here, so now let's talk about what you want, and how you're going to go about getting it.

Remember that *every moment of your life, you're in motion*. That's a universal law--nothing is simply standing still except maybe *relative* to something else (hence, the law of relativity). You are in motion right now. You might feel as if you're sitting still reading this book, but really you are hurtling through the universe at over 65,000 miles per hour, and that's not even taking into account the movement of the Earth spinning on its axis (if you're close to the equator, you're spinning at about 1,000 miles per hour). Of course, again, this is all calculated according to the laws of relativity.

But let's forget about the laws of relativity and the universe for a moment...let's look at it on a smaller level...the smallest level we can. Imagine we're looking at a living substance under a microscope. It's moving. It's always moving. Nothing is really sitting still. It might appear as though things are sitting still, but that's just another mortal illusion.

The Slayer knows that everything is always in constant motion.
That's the law.

With this law in mind, you must remember that every moment of every day, you are either moving *towards* what it is that you really want, or you're moving *away* from it. There is no standing still.

There is no *neutrality* in the universe--None.

There are positive charges and negative charges; there is light and there is darkness; and you are either moving towards your destiny or away from it every moment of every day. The real purpose of this lesson is to make you more conscious of this truth. As a Potential, you have to be more aware than you were *before* you were chosen. You have to remember that every moment of the day you are making a choice, and that choice, whatever it may be, is bringing you closer to your destiny, or farther away from it. Let me repeat that, so we're clear:

Slayer Principle:
Every moment of every day you are making a choice that will bring you
either closer to, or farther away from, your destiny.

That's a fact *and the truth.*

A Slayer is constantly stretching and working out his or her attitudinal muscles. Every person you meet from now on is your assignment. In case you skimmed over that part, let me repeat it:

Slayer Principle:
Every person you meet from now on is your assignment.

Every person you meet from now on will have been delivered to you to help you achieve your highest potential as a Slayer. Don't waste even one more encounter. You might not immediately learn the lesson; you might just understand what it was in retrospect, but every person you meet you were meant to meet, and you will meet every person you are meant to meet. Every person you meet is your teacher from now on. That means everyone--from the cashier at the grocery store, to the receptionist at the office, to your boss, to the toll-booth man. Don't waste even one more encounter.

So with all of this in mind, I would now like you to finish the following sentences:

I want _____.

&

I will _____.

BEWARE: Once you have done this, there is no turning back. You will have finished your Personal Compass. You will have a tool that few people have. You will have power that few people have, and you will from this moment on be accountable, as few people are. Just as Adam and Eve saw their own nakedness after eating the apple (according to the story), there will be no turning back. You will from this moment on be more aware of when you're doing right **by you**, and when you're not. You will be more aware of whether you're moving towards your destiny, or away from it, and you will be aware that you are the one in the driver's seat. With this awareness comes much burden. It is a gift that you give yourself, but as in life:

Your gift is your curse and your curse is your gift.

Only you can decide which it will be to you at any moment.

Here's how you might go about filling in the **I want _____** and **I will _____** sentences:

Ask yourself what it really is that you want out of life. I don't mean just today, but every day. What do you want? Peace? Happiness? To find meaning? Excitement? To leave a legacy? What?

I'll tell you what I wrote in the first time I made my Personal Compass:

"I want financial independence."

Notice how I didn't say a specific amount of money. I simply wanted to be free financially. I didn't want to worry about money. I knew that that my financial state had a direct impact on my mental state. I realize that money can't buy you happiness, but I also know this truth--**I can't be happy without it**. I really dig Mother Theresa, for example. She didn't tell us to send the poor *good vibrations*. She told us to send them **money**. I'm a big believer in getting your finances straight, and breaking the financial shackles that most of us have put on ourselves.

Let me take a moment to elaborate on this, because if you choose *not* to put anything regarding money in your Personal Compass, the odds of your financial situation changing are very slim, and that would not be good for you if room for improvement currently exists. Even if you are financially stable, there is normally room for improvement. Let me elaborate a little bit.

Picture this: you're sitting at your desk at work, and you have it in your mind that you work "for" someone rather than work "with" someone. You hear a little "Ding!" and see that you have a new email. You open that email, and it's from your "boss" and it only has three words on it.

You know the words.

They're the worst three words you can ever read on a Post-it Note, or email from your boss. Yup, *those* words:

"Come see me."

I'll bet you became a little queasy just now—when you read or heard those words —didn't you? That's because they cause a visceral (or *gut*) reaction. We'll talk more about other words that do the same, later.

This why having something about money in your Personal Compass is so important. If you're not financially independent (which means different things to different people) that will impact every relationship in your life. Frustration and fear will seep its way into the relationship you have with your significant other, with your coworkers, with your children, with your friends, and with yourself. It attacks your self-talk.

If you are living paycheck-to-paycheck, you will walk down the hallway to your boss' office thinking, "Omigod, what is it now? I feel sick. I need this paycheck," and other things along those lines. You will walk into your boss' office from a position of weakness, and it will show, because real weakness can never be hidden.

If, however, you had, let's say, a 6-month *"forget you"* fund in the bank (remember, it's just as easy to be six months ahead as it is to be six months behind), and were someone who truly invests in himself or herself, you would walk down the hallway thinking something more along the lines of, "**I am here for**

one reason: personal and professional development, and if for whatever reason, it comes to light in today's meeting that I will no longer be able to get that here, that's OK. With a happy heart, I can leave, and take time to find another place to work. I have the skills that people want; I am confident in my abilities and secure in my situation."

If you walk in with *that* attitude, the conversation that would follow would obviously be dramatically different from one that would have ensued if you were worried about getting that paycheck at the end of the week. This is why before slaying anything, we must go through this process of strengthening ourselves.

Of course, only you can choose what should be in **your**, "I want _____" sentences, but make sure you take your time and do what's necessary to make them as complete as possible. And be sure and write down as many statements as possible. Remember that putting something in writing really creates magic. When people first started writing down what they wanted, the words were called "spells" and the people who wrote them were called "wizards" because the things that they wrote down tended to come to pass—more often than the wishes of the people around them—the wishes that people around them were merely *thinking* about. Now I'm going to give you a habit of a Slayer—a habit that you must make your own. Get ready, because I'm about to **give you a secret:**

> *A Slayer has something to write with and something to write on at all times-- always always always. No exceptions.*

You should have something next to your bed, in the bathroom, in the kitchen, at your desk, in your bag. Whenever you think of something you'd like to add to your Personal Compass--write it down.

Now, before going any further, stop and write down at least 10 "I want _____" statements.

I mean now. You can use the workbook that goes with this book (page 4 in the workbook).

Ok, I'm going to assume that now you have your 10 statements. **It will not serve you to read another word if you don't have them**, so if you tend to read-ahead as most Slayers do, stop now and finish those sentences.

I mean it.

OK, now all that's left to do is finish your, "I will _____" statements.

Think of all that you have done so far. You have decided who you are, why you are here, and what you want. You are already leaps and bounds ahead of most people in terms of self-development. Most people couldn't finish the sentence, "I am _____" to save their lives. That's OK. That's why the world needs Slayers. That's why this course found you.

Your "I will _____" statements are the culmination of everything that we have done so far. Once you know *who you are*, how will that affect *what you will do*? Once you know *why you're here*, how will that affect *what you will do*? Once you know *what you want*, how will that affect *what you will do*? Going back to what we discussed at the beginning of this lesson, from now on, every moment of the day you have a choice. You will be more conscious of moving towards or away from your destiny. Every person you meet is your assignment, and that person will either usher you towards or away from your destiny. From now on, the choice is yours, and your actions will start changing.

What does this person you have described, **do**? What does this person whose purpose you have described, **do**? What does this person who wants what you've described, **do**?

For example, in my Personal Compass, I have things such as, "I will practice patience and kindness with every person I meet. I will transform my environment, and make it more beautiful wherever I go. I will cast light into darkness. I will separate facts from truth."

The reason the, "I will _____" statements are so important is because there will be times where you will be so challenged, you might lose your mind for a moment. If you thought that you have encountered difficult people before, ***watch out***. Once you have decided (remember, decide comes from the Latin *decidere*, meaning to cut off--you will be cutting off all other options, once you have ***decided***), and proclaimed to the world that you are the next Slayer, what you *once* thought of as difficult people will seem like little golden retriever puppies, or monarch butterflies. Once you proclaim that you are a Slayer, you will be tested more than ever. The Energy Vampires will come with more power, and they will come more frequently.

The difference between now and before, however, is that now you will have further developed your Slayer powers. Do not, however, make the mistake that many Potentials make, and think that you can breeze over making your Personal Compass, or that you can just make it in your head.

Don't even think about it.

The time is coming soon when you'll be confronted with a horrific Energy Vampire, and you will need to use your Personal Compass. You will need it because you will become emotionally out-of-control. You might be a Potential, but you are also a human being, and human beings have emotions, and emotions sometimes go out-of-control. Remember this truth:

Out-of-control emotions make smart people stupid.

That's a fact and the truth. Later in this course we'll talk more about the brain, and the role it plays in our slaying, but suffice it to say: If you have a human brain, and I'm assuming you do, you have emotions. When the right side of our brain (the emotional side) is activated, it draws us out of the left side (logic) and we forget things like *who we are, and why we're really here*. I'm sure you've experienced this some time when you were talking to your most beloved, and you said awful, horrific things while you were emotionally charged, and then later had to apologize, and said something like, "I don't know why I said that. I didn't mean it."

I know you didn't mean it, and I know why you said it: You were on drugs. The emotions caused your brain to swell with so many drugs, you might as well have been on PCP. That, coupled with being drawn out of the left side of your brain, made you certifiably crazy and stupid.

That's a fact and the truth.

This is why you need a Personal Compass. Thankfully, by the time you are done with this lesson, you will have completed yours. You will use your compass when emotions are running high. From now on, during any situation in which you find yourself getting heated, you are to **stop** before you say or do **ANYTHING**. Stop, and refer to your Personal Compass, and recite it. It will remind you who you are, why you're here, what you want, and how to get it. Never forget that it is the EV's job to get you to forget all of that, and become an EV yourself.

You will no longer fall prey to that trap.

You will have the necessary tools.

You will have your Personal Compass.

Make it.

You will need it.

Frequently.

If you need additional help completing your Personal Compass, refer to the workbook in the back of this book.

Once you've completed this lesson, you can proceed to lesson four. If you need any help, please feel free to visit our website at www.powerdiversity.com where you'll find tons of useful tools—all free-- for dealing with negativity in the workplace, including videos, audios, links, blogs, advice columns, and many others resources.

Good luck. Until our next lesson…

Homework:
- Complete pages 4 and 5 of the ENERGY VAMPIRE SLAYING: 101 WORKBOOK.
- For the next 24 hours, when you are confronted with a negative person or a negative environment, physically touch your Personal Compass quick-reference flash-card (this means you must keep it handy at all times) and recite as many statements as you can.
- Complete your Personal Compass on pages 6-7 of the ENERGY VAMPIRE SLAYING: 101 WORKBOOK, sign it, and frame it. Once you've done this, place it somewhere where you'll see it every day from now on.
- Choose one of the ***Slayer Principles*** cards that accompany this program, and carry it around with you for 24 hours. Pull it out and read it out loud at least 5 times throughout the day.

For the resources that go with this and other chapters, including audio recordings and quick-reference cards, go to http://powerdiversity.com/the-library

Chapter 4: Why out of control emotions make smart people stupid, and what you can do about it

You've made it all the way to lesson four already? Way to go! You should now have a Personal Compass, which is one of the most powerful tools any communicator can have (and less than 1% of people have actually created). You are now in an *elite* group of communicators.

Remember, if you have not actually completed lessons 1 through 3, which detail writing your Personal Compass, **STOP RIGHT NOW** and do it. To become a Slayer takes time and dedication, and no lessons can be skipped or skimmed over.

That said, assuming that you have completed all of the preceding lessons, you are now ready for tactical verbal training, or

Verbal Tactics for Slayers

The art of verbal tactics, or engaging in tactical communication, is all about staying (and *slaying*) in the **response** mode. Let's take a minute and review this concept.

Any savvy communicator will tell you that the trick to staying in the power position is being able to remain in the *response* mode rather than the *reaction* mode. The reaction mode is, basically, first thing into the brain = first thing out of the mouth. We all *begin* in the reaction mode. Some people forever *stay* in the reaction mode. Those who stay in the reaction mode will never be called to be Slayers as you have been called. **You cannot be a Slayer while in the reaction mode.** There comes a time in a Slayer's development when he or she realizes that the first thing into the brain = the **worst** thing out of the mouth.

As communicators, we are all someplace on the following scale:

STOPPABLE   UNSTOPPABLE

*Where are **you**?*

Furthermore, there are **two** types of *stoppable* communicators: Those who at times are totally at a loss for words because of what others say, and those who may be able to easily fire back, but do it in an *unenlightened* way. For example, some people are speechless when confronted with Energy Vampires; they literally struggle to find *any* words. Others respond to Energy Vampires by **engaging** them. What I mean by that is, let's say an Energy Vampire (namely a *Sniper*) says something to you such as, "Nice outfit! Where are you going? To the prom???" and you are quick to reply with some equally unenlightened insult. This does not mean you are *unstoppable*, but rather *stoppable*--the EV got you to stop being who you really are, and conform to the situation rather than transform the situation. *This is not the way of the Slayer.*

Slayer Principle:

What Energy Vampires say and do is about them, and a reflection of them. What you say and do is about you and a reflection of you.

The Slayer is a different kind of *unstoppable* from what most people are accustomed to. You might be good at insulting people *back*. You might be good at being *aggressive* (which is different, of course, from being assertive). If someone pushes the wrong buttons, you might even be able to magically transform into a giant, fire-breathing Energy Vampire yourself. Some people are even proud that they can quickly hurt people; they do it to entertain themselves and others.

But why would you ever want to do that? Why would you ever want to BE that person?

Of course, mortal illusions push us to the point where we actually buy into the delusion, and become difficult people ourselves. We lose our temper, our brain starts to release chemicals that drug us to the point of basically *tripping out*, and we forget our real purpose; we become Energy Vampires. It's happened to the best of us.

It happens far less to a Slayer.

Even when someone comes at you with darkness, it is your duty as a Slayer to respond with light. Remember--**light casts out darkness.** You have to be that light, and you *can* be that light. *Things change when they are brought to light.* Things look different in the light because you *see* differently in the light. When confronting difficult people, it is **you** who choose to either stay in the dark or bring those people into the light. Energy Vampires, like regular vampires, hate the light, and can't live in it.

Slayer Principle:

Light casts out darkness.

This principle is important to remember, because difficult co-workers, aggravating customers, and obnoxious in-laws will always exist. What will change is the ***ending*** of the story--how you feel walking away after having dealt with difficult people. The ending of our encounters with EVs tends to be the same again and again until we experience some sort of turning point, and recognize the need for change. Our lives in general tend to be that way, right? Cycle-cycle-cycle-cycle-TURNING POINT.

I'm going to assume you've had such a turning point or you wouldn't be reading these words right now. That's why this book landed in your hands at this moment, *wouldn't you agree*?

It would be foolish, however to think that you will *always* be able to respond with power, confidence, and enlightenment *on the fly*. People say things to us that we don't expect. People ask us crazy questions. People do strange things! How are we supposed to be in the response mode all the time? Of course, it's a process getting there. Maybe out of the 100 chances to get it right, you got it right twice today. Well, If you have a few more tactics *tomorrow* than you had *today*, you might get it right **three** times tomorrow, and maybe 5 times by the end of the week! Even if, by strengthening your communication and dealing with difficult people skills, you get it right *just one more time*, that's OK. It will be **the one time it really counts.** Trust me.

The first thing any Slayer needs in his or her verbal arsenal to help stay in the response mode, even while under pressure, is a set of good **magic power phrases**.

Whether dealing with difficult people at work, slaying Energy Vampires, or simply polishing your communication skills, you must have a good, basic set of magic power phrases in your verbal arsenal. Even though they may seem simple, they are powerful, and are used almost exclusively by master communicators and Energy Vampire Slayers.

Are you ready for your first set of **4 magic power phrases**?

OK, take a deep breath...

Now say these out loud:

1) **That's interesting; tell me more.**

2)   **That's interesting; why would you ask that?**

3) **That's interesting; why would you say that? &**

4) **That's interesting; why would you do that?**

With these four phrases, you should be able to *respond* rather than *react* to just about anything. Again, getting out of the reaction mode and into the response mode is fundamental to developing your Slayer skills. Having magic power phrases ready such as these will immediately help you to respond, rather than react, when people say things that might otherwise have caught you off guard or left you speechless. The trick is to start practicing them now. You have to be able to rattle them off in your sleep.

STOP RIGHT NOW and read those four phrases out loud again, 4 times each.

Check out the quick-reference flash-cards that accompany this book. You should carry either this book--or the card with these phrases on it--around with you until you've had a chance to use each one of those power phrases at least twice. Look for opportunities to use them. The ability to fire off a question, thereby throwing the "communication ball" back into your opponent's court is a highly developed (and highly coveted) skill. You can fast-track yourself through the learning process by simply quickly learning a few good verbal tactics such as these.

Now it's time for another crucial principle--are you ready? Take another deep breath:

Slayer Principle:

Every person you meet from now on is your assignment.

Remember that every person you meet you are supposed to meet, and you will meet every person you are supposed to meet. Everyone is a teacher, everyone is a lesson. Practice everything you can, with everyone you can, as often as you can.

The tactics and scripts in this book are all meant to be mastered and used immediately. You should start looking for opportunities to practice them, and do so often. Even if it appears to be a simple tactic, **practice it**. You want to practice even the things in this book that might seem easy, because when a human being is assaulted or attacked physically or verbally, their brains start to go out of balance.

Let's review this.

Thousands of years of programming and hard-wiring have gone into making your brain what it is today. It is really what you do everything with, as well as what you *see* with--as opposed to your eyes--and it gets cloudy when you are attacked.

When you are attacked, a bio-chemical reaction is triggered, namely the "fight or flight" response. Discovered by Harvard physiologist Walter Cannon, this response is hard-wired into our brains and is designed to protect us from harm. This response happens in the area of our brain called the hypothalamus, which—when stimulated—prompts a sequence of nerve cell firing and chemical releases that prepares our body for either fighting or running.

When our fight or flight response is activated, chemicals such as adrenaline, noradrenaline and cortisol are released into our bloodstream. This chemical release causes dramatic changes in our body. Our respiratory rate increases. Blood is pumped away from our digestive tract and into our muscles and limbs, so we can use them for running and/or fighting. Our pupils dilate. Our awareness intensifies. Our sight sharpens. Our impulses quicken. Our perception of pain diminishes. Our immune system even mobilizes. We become prepared— physically and psychologically—for a dramatic event. Even our animal instinct to "hunt to kill" the enemy kicks in.

You can see where this would lead to problems for even the most enlightened Slayer.

When our fight or flight system is activated, we tend to see everything in our environment as a possible threat to our survival. The fight or flight system overrides the left-hand side of the brain—where our logic and developed beliefs reside--and moves us into an emotional (right-brained) "attack" mode. Because we have moved into *savage* survival mode, we tend to see everyone and everything as a possible enemy and we overreact out of emotion. Our fear is exaggerated and our thinking distorted. Because we actually see with our brains, when our brain is out of whack, we literally can't see straight. We see things differently. Literally and figuratively.

Slayer Principle:

Out of control emotions make sane people crazy, and smart people stupid.

That's a biological fact, and the truth.

Let's review some brain basics. Basically, the brain has two sides, or h*emispheres*--the left hemisphere and the right hemisphere.

Logic   Emotion

Facts   Creativity

Numbers   Concepts

Memory   Imagination

Language   Empathy

To break it down simply, as illustrated above, you can see the left side of the brain is where things such as logic, facts, numbers, memory, and language live. Incidentally, the left side of the brain is generally considered to be the more "male" side. Most men are more *left-brain* oriented. The right side of the brain is where things such as emotion, creativity, concepts, imagination, and empathy live. Most women are more *right-brain* oriented, thus the right side of the brain is generally considered to be the more "female" side. Regardless of your sex, you are going to be either more left-brain or right-brain dominant.

*If you're saying to yourself, "No, I'm really balanced, I'm more whole-brained, and you can't put me in a box like that," **lighten up**--it's a generalization for example's sake.*

35

Although all of us use both our left *and* our right hemispheres, each of us has more **dominant** sides and traits. While we are all combinations of different thinking and communication styles, it is important to recognize the dominant traits in both ourselves and others. Once we can do this, we can start to more consciously shift our language to suit the communication style of others. This is what is called implementing The Platinum Rule.

The Platinum Rule is very different from The Golden Rule. Most people practice the golden rule with *great* intentions. To review, The Golden Rule is, "Treat others as you would like to be treated."

DON'T DO THAT!

Instead, we should be practicing the Platinum Rule, which is, "Treat others the way *THEY* would like to be treated." It sounds simple, and for some of us it sounds like a *preposterous* idea, but trust me, this is a fundamental principle of slaying. To put it another way, when you're communicating with other people, "Speak their language" and you'll get better results.

PLATINUM RULE:

Treat others the way THEY would like to be treated.

Keep this rule in mind, and what this idea means to you until our next lesson. As you go through your day, when you encounter people, especially difficult people, think to yourself, "How can I more effectively speak *this* person's language?"

Later in this chapter, you will learn how to use coping statements and hemisphere switching to keep control when the emotional side of your brain wants to take over from the logical—and leave you wordless and stupid and out-of-control.

Slayer Principle:

The better someone feels around you, the more power you *both* have.

Keeping this principle in mind, you will find that the brain is going play a major role in you Energy Vampire slaying. Once you are more tactical with your words, your tone, and your approach when dealing with difficult people, and once you *style-shift* to more effectively speak their language, you will actually be affecting their brain chemistry.

Isn't that cool? You can actually have control of how you affect other people's brain chemistry. You've actually experienced this before. You know how when you're with some people, they make you feel good, and energetic. It's as if they are giving you a jolt of happiness right into your veins. Then there are those people who make you feel so awful, it's as if they're giving you downers the whole time you're with them. The truth is that the people we're around *really do* affect us on a chemical level, a conscious level, a subconscious level, a genetic level, and even on an atomic level. What you are going to do is be more conscious of this, and use it to your advantage.

If you're looking to "get through" to a right-brain dominant person, for example, you must *speak to* the emotional side of the brain, using emotional language. This is more difficult for you if you are left-brain oriented (or l-directed). If you want to connect with someone who is left-brain oriented, and you are more right-brain oriented (or r-directed) then this is more difficult for you. The trick is to realize how what we say to *ourselves* and what we say to others affects the brain, and the resulting behavior.

Almost everything we know about the human brain has been discovered in the past 50 years. We are still just beginning to understand how the brain really works, and how we can work with it more effectively. For example, we now know for a fact that there is certain language that stimulates right-brain activity, and language that stimulates left-brain activity. Remember that when you go into tactical mode, you must be aware what side of the brain you should be speaking to, how to speak to it, and when.

Let's start, however, with our own brains. We talk to ourselves more than we talk to anyone else, after all.

The average person speaks at the rate of about 150 words per-minute. The world's fastest talker speaks at the rate of about 600 words per-minute. You speak to yourself at the rate of about 800 words per-minute. We don't really think in abstract thoughts; we talk to ourselves. This is called, naturally, our self-talk.

Unfortunately, most of us have ineffective speech patterns that we use when talking to ourselves. To get superior results, we must first master our own **self-talk**.

The more we learn about the brain, and the more we develop computers, the more we see that the two of them work in quite similar ways. For example, if you're programming a computer, you must use very specific language, or coding, to get the results you're looking for. If you use the right code, you get results; if you use the wrong code, you get poor results or no results. It's the same with our brains.

Let's say, for example that you are on a first date, or in a job interview, or someone says something to you that really strikes a nerve, and you feel like crying, but the *LAST* thing you want to do at that moment is cry. What would you say to yourself to hold back the tears?

Quick-what would you say?

If you said, "Don't cry, or I'm not going to cry," I'll bet you cry a lot.

Or imagine that someone is pushing your buttons and making you angry, but you don't want to explode. What do you say to yourself that actually gets results? "Don't get angry, don't let him get to you, I'm not going to explode" won't get you anywhere. Why? It's not the right *code* your brain needs to generate results.

Study after study has been done showing how our self-talk affects our behavior and the results we get (or fail to get) in life. One of my favorites was the study that concluded that Nascar drivers (the ones who drive around the race track at speeds reaching nearly 200 mph) are actually *more likely* to crash into the wall around the track if they say to themselves, "I'm not going to hit the wall." Why? Because they're not giving their brain the right code—the code to get the results they seek.

Of course, I realize that there is no "delete" button for our emotions. We can, however, have some control over them, and can have more control than the average person if we simply learn tactics such as ***coping statements***, and ***hemisphere switching***. In other words, coping statements and hemisphere switching will give us the code our brains need for positive self-talk.

Slayer Principle:

Slayers know how to use coping statements and how to hemisphere switch to prevent the right side of the brain from overtaking the left.

Coping statements are phrases that you practice and memorize for emergency situations. Remember, you don't want to have to think too hard in an emergency situation, because by its very nature, an emergency situation will logically mentally disable you. This is because *becoming* emotionally charged *draws you out* of the logical side of the brain.

Most of us say things to ourselves such as, "I'm not going to cry," and then get even more frustrated with ourselves for crying. Or "Slow down; don't hit the wall," and then we CRASH into the wall. Remember, our brains process information in a manner similar to computers--garbage in=garbage out. You must give your brain the information "coded" the right way for results. That's what coping statements help us do.

There are 2 critical components to a coping statement:
1- It is positively phrased.
2- It is in the present.

As you can see, if you say to yourself, "I'm not going to cry," as most people do, that's the *opposite* of a coping statement; it's negatively phrased, and it's future tense. You can't tell a computer what not to do in the future; you'll get nothing. The same is true for our brains. You can't tell your brain or yourself what not to do in the future and expect to get any results. You have to tell yourself ***what you are right now***. For example, if you want to make it easy, just begin your coping statements with, "**I am___**" phrases. Instead of, "I'm not going to cry," what you mean to say is, "I am strong." Instead of, "I'm not going to get angry," what you mean to say is, "I am cool, calm, and collected." If you are a Nascar driver, you might try: "I am an excellent, experienced driver" when you see that wall coming. Those are coping statements.

Remember to practice coping statements before you need them (there are some great handy-reference cards in the back of this book) so that when you need them, you don't have to think about it. Remember--**it's most difficult to think of a good coping statement at the time you need it the most.**

Once you've learned the nature of coping statements, it's time to hemisphere switch.

Hemisphere switching is consciously stimulating one side of the brain, which draws us out of the other side. The vast majority of the time, when one side of the brain is stimulated, the other side's stimulation dies down. This is important to understand when it comes to hemisphere switching. The more we use the logical side of our brain--for example, if we're doing algebra--the more it draws energy and activity out of the emotional side of the brain. The more emotional we are, the more we are drawn out of the logical side of the brain. This simple but accurate description of how our brains basically work should explain why out-of-control emotions make smart people stupid and sane people crazy.

Most of us have had the experience where an emergency occurs, and we suddenly lose our senses. We have trouble remembering where the phone is, and when we find it, we have trouble using it. The right--emotional--side of our brain is so stimulated, that we get *sucked out* of the left side of the brain, and we have trouble accessing things that live there. For example, if you have trouble finding the words in an emotionally-charged situation, it's because when you are emotional, you are sucked out of the side of the brain where the words live.

I believe the most extreme example of being drawn out of logic because of right-brain stimulation is falling in love. **You are never as stupid as you are when you first fall in love,** and the phenylethlamine (the love drug) is produced by the brain in buckets. You literally see things that aren't there. You hallucinate. You might as well be on PCP. Other people wonder what "you two" "see" in each other, because the other people are not suffering from severe right-brain stimulation. They aren't blinded by emotion—such as two people in love (aka infatuation) are. (Of course in time, this stimulation begins to wane, and that's when people in love see one another for who they are—warts and all—and sometimes "fall out" of love—because the blinders have been removed.) If love problems are troubling you at the moment, that's an entirely different course. If you're suffering in love, go to the "HELP ME DAN" section of our website. In most other emotional cases, however, hemisphere switching will definitely help you get back into that left side of your brain, and in so doing, will draw you out of the emotional side.

(By the way, did you know that there are things you can do to release phenylethlamine in the brains of other people? Yup. That, however, is an advanced Slayer tactic for which you are not yet ready.)

I'll help you develop your hemisphere switching powers with this simple 2-step tactic:

HEMISPHERE SWITCHING 101:
1-Lift your chin up
2-Recite your phone number backwards including the area code

Step number one: Lift your chin up. Children have the ability to throw their heads back and really have a good cry. Adults, however, can't do that. When adults need to really let loose and bawl, they put their heads down and cry. Think about when people really sob—you know--like on those talk shows where people learn who the baby's daddy really is. When people let loose and cry, they put their heads down. That's the physiological norm. Psychological changes yield physiological changes. Just as that is true, *physiological* changes can yield *psychological* changes as well.

When people lose control, it's common to offer them a drink of water, right? That's not to hydrate them; drinking water forces people to lift their chin up (thus the expression, "keep your chin up") which causes a physiological change in the brain, and helps to keep emotions under control.

Step number two: Recite your phone number backwards including the area code. Now, figure out what's 13 x 7. Stop reading and do it right now--and recite your phone number backwards, including the area-code, as well. DO IT.

Chances are your eyes just shifted to the left a little bit while you were thinking. That's because the information you were looking for--things like numbers and math--live in the left side of your brain, and when we access one side or another, our eyes naturally gravitate towards the side we're accessing.

HOT TIP:

Observing the eyes is one technique law enforcement agents and other "interrogators" (including grandmothers) use to determine whether people are telling the truth or lying. When you ask someone a question such as, "What time did you come in last night, and what were you doing?" watch the eyes of the person to whom you're speaking. The direction in which they move is very telling. If you ask someone where they were last night and they look to the left as they think, what side of the brain did their eyes move towards? Logical; memory...probably the truth. If you ask someone where they were and they look to the right, what side of the brain did their eyes move towards? Creative--that's right--they're dreaming up a good one for you. Keep that under your hat. It's a great Slayer tactic. My grandmother taught me this long before I confirmed it scientifically.... And my mother was a master. I thought she was a mind-reader before I discovered she was an eye (and therefore brain) reader. If only I knew then what I know now, I could have gotten away with much much more!

As you further your training, you'll learn more techniques such as the ones you learned in today's lesson, but for now it's time to stop and practice what you've learned.

Good luck. Until our next lesson....

Homework:

- Review your Personal Compass frequently throughout the day, and especially when you feel yourself getting upset in any way
- Complete page 8 of the ENERGY VAMPIRE SLAYING: 101 WORKBOOK.
- Practice using the 4 magic power phrases you learned in this chapter
- Remember every person is your assignment
- Implement The Platinum Rule whenever you can
- Practice using coping statements
- Practice hemisphere switching
- Notice where people's eyes go when you ask them questions
- Choose a new Slayer Principle from the Slayer Principle cards, and carry it with you for the next 24 hours. Review it at least 5 times throughout the day.

You must do all the above in preparation for your next lesson. You might want to read ahead, and that's OK. If you do read ahead, however, after you put this book down, you must come back to it starting at chapter 5, having done the homework listed above.

You have done a great job so far. The upcoming lessons will require a lot of brain power and strength, so go rest, young Slayer, and we shall resume our training later.

For the resources that go with this and other chapters, including audio recordings and quick-reference cards, go to http://powerdiversity.com/the-library

Chapter 5: Watch your words

You're really serious aren't you? Most Potentials don't make it this far. I'm proud of you. You truly do have potential as a Slayer.

I'm assuming that you've done all the preceding lessons. If you have somehow arrived here without doing lessons 1-4, STOP and do them. **The lessons that follow will do you no good unless you have already completed the lessons and homework assignments from the first four lessons.**

Now, assuming that's done...

DANGER DANGER DANGER!

There are words you are using that rob you of effectiveness, and actually sabotage your success as a Slayer. As you know, most people throw words around haphazardly, without any regard to the real effect words have on the world, and the people in it. Not Slayers. Slayers know that words are the most powerful things people have. Words are what cause wars, and words are what bring peace. Words are what build people up or tear people down. Words are what propel us from one class to another, and words have the power to bring us from darkness to light. Even most *creation* stories tell the tale that we were "spoken" into existence.

Sticks and stones might break my bones, but words will never hurt me? Nothing could be more untrue.

Most communication training courses tell us that every message that we send face-to-face is made up of three basic components:

Words: 7%
Tone: 38%
Body Language: 55%

I believe, as I'm sure you do, that this is over-simplifying things a bit. First of all, we rarely communicate face-to-face anymore (this is actually quite a shame), and secondly, we all know that it only takes **one word** to make or break our message, and sabotage our success.

Take the work of Doctor Emoto, for example. If you Google "Dr. Emoto water Images" you'll find examples of how our words affect water on a *molecular* level. According to Emoto's theories, the bottom line is, if you say pretty things to a glass of water as the water freezes, the water crystals look pretty under a microscope. If you say ugly things to a glass of water as the water freezes, the crystals look ugly under a microscope. The glass of water still looks the same on the outside, but it changes forever on the inside, on a level that can't be seen by the human eye. Of course, there's much more to it than that, but that's the principle. Our words have the power to literally transform things and people.

I have not personally performed the experiments Dr. Emoto describes in his books, but I don't need to. I've seen his theory in action. Human beings are made up of about 70% water. Coincidentally, so is the Earth, and so are the cells within our body--further evidence of the

Slayer Principle:

What's true on any level is true on every level.

Most of us can remember a time where we were minding our own business, maybe at the dinner table, and someone said something to us. Something hurtful. Maybe that person called us a name. Maybe they told us we don't *really* need another serving, or maybe they simply teased us. It might have been a sentence, or it might have been just one word. The person who said it didn't think about it beforehand, or while saying it, and probably has never thought about it since. We, however, have thought about what they said every single day, and will probably think about it every day until we die. It has become part of the permanent track that plays in our head--our self-talk, contributing to who we are. It has become part of us--changing us *on the inside*. We haven't been the same sine the moment the words were spoken.

When it happened, however, we still looked like the same glass of water on the outside.

The point is, while you might be able to argue the effects that words have on water, plants, and other things, you cannot argue the truth that they tremendously affect *people*, which brings us to the next

Slayer Principle:

Words are the most powerful things that exist. They are what create and destroy.

If you are serious about being a Slayer, you must always keep this principle in mind, and remember that if your intention is to destroy with your words, what you will end up destroying is yourself. Whatever effect your words have on others will have the exact same effect on you. It is an impossibility that you affect others without having the same effect on yourself. This is why it is your duty to study words and language patterns--**out of self interest.**

Slayer Principle:

Your words will have the same effect *on you* as they do *on others*.

Words are what bring war, and words are what bring peace.
Words are what cultivate love, and words are what cultivate hate.
Words are what resurrect, and words are what crucify.
Words are what cast light, and words are what cast darkness.

Words do everything.

Slayer Principle:

If you have the right words, you can do anything.

This is why the Slayer chooses words wisely, and studies words.

At this time in your Slayer development, a simple and effective way to improve your verbal prowess is to keep a **danger phrase** and **power phrase** list. This is one of the most powerful tools you'll use, and you should use it frequently. A danger phrase/power phrase template is included with the quick-reference cards in the back of this book. Use it, add to it, and reference it every day.

Danger phrases are words and phrases that we should purge from our verbal repertoire. There are many reasons why these words and phrases end up on a danger phrase list. They could be phrases that sabotage our communication success and deliver something other than the result we desire when we say them; they could be words that rob us of communication power; they could be phrases that cause a toxic bio-chemical reaction in others' brains; they could be words that carry such a negative vibration, they simply should not be passing through our lips. Starting today, you will begin to purge these danger phrases from your speech patterns.

ALERT!ALERT!ALERT!ALERT!ALERT!

From this point forward, when you identify a danger phrase as one you use, you must write it down on your danger phrase list, along with a power phrase to use as its replacement. If there is no replacement for the phrase, label it "delete phrase."

If you are replacing a danger phrase with a power phrase, write them both down, and **repeat the power phrase ten times out loud**. Keeping a danger/power phrase list is not an optional part of your development. In order for you to master the skills that you'll need to reach your potential, it is a requirement. You must constantly add to this list. Once you do this, you will find yourself moving from the *reaction* mode and into the *response* mode more often, and more effortlessly.

As a matter of fact...here's what is going to happen. Are you ready? *Take a breath...*

Part of your homework is going to be to write down a few danger phrases, and maybe some power phrases. Within 72 hours of doing so, you will have the opportunity to reference that list--guaranteed!

Here's what will happen: a master teacher will appear to you in the form of a difficult person, and you will be on the verge of using a danger phrase, when suddenly you'll stop, and you'll shift from the *reaction* mode, into the *response,* mode, and you'll use a *power phrase* instead. You will get a different, better result from the one you're accustomed to, and in that moment, you'll stop and think to yourself, "Oh my gosh, it's true...I did it...it worked," or something along those lines.

It is in that moment that you will begin to see the true greatness of your powers.

You might know that you have *some* personal power, but you never *really* know how powerful you are until you start exercising that power **on a daily basis, in a positive way**. That is what you'll be doing throughout this training. You will develop an entirely new understanding of the role you play in every one of your relationships, and you will begin to more deeply understand and believe the

Slayer Principle:

You are in charge of every relationship in your life.

Again, although you might find it hard to believe, you are in charge of, and responsible for, the outcome of **every single** communication situation in which you find yourself.

Furthermore, if you speak to people the same way you spoke to them yesterday, you will get the same results as you got yesterday. If you get the same results as you got yesterday, you will have the same experience you had yesterday. Your experience yesterday wasn't perfect, or you wouldn't be reading this book. Although it might be different for you to keep lists and use verbal tactics such as the ones you'll find in this training, **you must do this in the manner that is outlined herein in order to achieve maximum result**. You must do different things to get different results. Yes, keeping lists and using tactics, such as the ones you'll learn in this training might be different for you, *but doing so will help you speak differently*, and *get better results immediately*.

An example of a danger phrase is "calm down," and I'd like you to write this on your new danger phrase list, whether you start by using the template included in this book, or make your own list from scratch. "Calm down" is a danger phrase because no one in the history of the world has ever heard it and calmed down as a result of hearing that phrase. In fact, it normally gets the opposite result from what we wanted, and the other person gets even more out of control as they tell us "Don't tell me to calm down!"

What we should be saying to get others to calm down when they are emotionally charged is a power phrase that begins with something along the lines of, "I understand..." Remember, when someone speaks to us from the emotional (right side) of the brain, we have to speak back to the emotional (right side) of the brain before they can get "*un-stuck*" and progress can be made. Some versions of, "I understand you're really upset," or, "I can see how frustrated you are," are good examples of power phrases we can use to replace "calm down."

That said, "I understand *how you feel*" is a **danger** phrase, because again, it tends to get people even more upset, and they think or say, "No you don't!" What we want to say to get the result we're looking for is, "I can understand **why** you feel that way." Adding the **why** changes the message, and tends to get the result we want. We're speaking to, and validating, the *right* side of the brain, which tends to calm people down so they can begin to think rationally and *hear* us. Adding the *why* changes the message from, "I have felt, or feel now, the same way that you feel right now," which tends to aggravate people, to "I can comprehend the chain of events that have led you to feel the way you currently feel. Not that I can relate, but I can understand why you feel the way you do." The latter is the message that most of us are trying to send, but fail because we aren't as precise as we could be with our words.

Slayers are precise. Slayers know how to "turn it on" using communication tools and tactics.

"No offense but," is another example of a danger phrase. In this case, it signals that you are about to say something that you know will be offensive, but you are going to say it anyway. **Slayers don't do that**. In this example, there would be no power phrase to replace this phrase. This is what we call a *delete phrase*, meaning it's a phrase that you should simply stop using. Furthermore, in this case, it also means that *you should not say* whatever it is you wanted to say following this phrase. If you know that someone is going to be offended by what you're about to say, it is your job to think of a way to deliver the message you believe needs to be delivered without offending the recipient. Or as a second option, simply do not deliver the message at all.

"Don't take this the wrong way, but..." is similar to, "No offense but..." in the sense that *the **wrong** way* will be exactly how they will take it, because it's exactly how you **mean** it; therefore, *it's the **right** way*, and the *wrong* message. As a general rule, remember that in terms of communication, a Slayer lives in a win-win universe, and can find a way to communicate that honors everyone at all times. Of course, sometimes we need to engage in assertive or even aggressive communication to protect ourselves or others, but when we are truly at our best and in the *Slayer zone*, a win-win is found even on what appears to be a communication battlefield.

"You need" and "I need" are also danger phrases. These are not delete phrases, but in general, should be avoided. For example, "You need to focus on this project," generally results in the thought or phrase, "*I don't need to do anything*!" Changing the phrase to, "This project deserves your full attention," changes the message, and the general result. "I need that project by the end of the day," is likely to evoke a, "yeah, well, I need a raise." More effective would be: "That report is due by the end of the day."

In general, when you begin a sentence with, "you need," the other person gets defensive, and when you begin it with, "I need," you appear needy. The remedy is to place **the powerful subject first**. Meaning--what is it in your message that deserves the most attention? In the preceding examples, it was the project, and the report. Yet, your needs, or the other person's obligations were placed at the beginning, or as the subject, of the sentences, where the **power** lives in sentences. In this example, once you place the project or report in its rightful place as the subject, you'll get the results you seek.

Choose your sentence subjects wisely. Remember—subjects are where the power resides in your sentences, and powerful communicators choose their subjects wisely.

"I'm sorry" is an example of a danger phrase that is simply a **delete** phrase. We all tend to say this phrase too often, and it decreases our personal power. Women tend to say it more than men do. You know who doesn't say it much at all? Powerful communicators and Energy Vampire Slayers. If you need to apologize, say the words, "I was wrong, and I apologize." This phrase holds a lot of weight, as opposed to, "I'm sorry," which holds almost no weight with anyone. Of course, "I'm sorry for your loss," would be an exception to this, and would be appropriate because the meaning of *sorry* in this context has nothing to do with an apology, but rather is a statement of concern for an event we did not cause (unless we just killed the person, of course….)

SLAYER SOCIAL EXPERIMENT:

Go to the grocery store, and "accidentally" bump other people's carts as you pass them. Watch how most men don't say anything, and how most women say, "I'm sorry" as **you** bump into **them.**

Don't be in that "sorry" group!

Just as sometimes we have danger phrases that do not have substitutes, or partners, we also have some power phrases that aren't replacing anything in particular. They are simply phrases that we use in a variety of different circumstances to achieve the desired communication result.

The phrase, "That may be, but" is an example of a good power phrase that isn't necessarily replacing anything, but you can tactically use during difficult communication situations. For example, let's say you're delivering a message to *The Victim* (we'll talk more about the different names Energy Vampires have, and how to identify and slay them in chapter 6) who is **full** of excuses. "That may be, but" is a great power phrase you can use to stay on message, as you respond to a litany of their problems and pain.

Slayer Principle:

Stay on message.

Victims try to throw us off message by giving us excuses and drama. You might, for example, tell them that their first appointment is at 9:00, and they are expected to be at their work station at that time. They might come back with something such as, "Yeah, but I have to take my son to school because his dad is in the hospital, and the bus doesn't come out to where we live, and I need to give him his medicine on the way to school..." You know the story. To help stay on message, you use the power phrase "That may be, but" and get right back to your point!

One mistake many of us make before our Slayer training is that we engage.

DON'T DO THAT!

Slayer Principle:

What gets rewarded gets repeated.

Many times difficult people repeat their difficult behavior simply because they get the payoff, or reward they're looking for from us. (They are engaging us in battle.) **What gets rewarded gets repeated.** Remember that the first time someone gossips with you, **that's about them.** The twentieth time someone gossips with you, **that's about you.** The first time someone manipulates you, that's about them. The twentieth time, that's about you. The first time someone dumps on you emotionally, that's about them. The twentieth time, that's about *you*. What gets rewarded gets repeated. Sometimes the reward we give, especially to victims, is that we *engage* them (or we allow them to engage us). We allow ourselves to be drawn into the drama.

Instead of engaging **The Victim**, try using a power phrase such as, "That may be, but..." along with the broken record, and it would sound something like this:

"Charlie, your first client is arriving at 9:00 tomorrow, and you're expected to be at your station, ready to assist her."

"But tomorrow I have to bring my son to school!"

"That may be, but you're expected to be at your station at 9:00 tomorrow."

"But his dad's in the hospital, so I'm the only one who can bring him!"

"That may be, but you're expected at 9:00 tomorrow."

"But the bus doesn't come out to our house, and I already told you this. I thought it was OK!"

"That may be but you're expected at 9:00 tomorrow."

Watch how quickly people get the message *when we stay on message.* Most people are very easily thrown off message. This is something that you must address and master, and having phrases such as, "that may be but…" coupled with tactics such as the broken record (repeating the very same thing over and over again, as often as necessary) can help you master staying on message quickly and easily.

There is another category of words that should be on your danger phrase list: **Words of death**. Words of death are words that should never be spoken or written ever again by anyone. Words of death are words that have been used to label people or groups of people, and these same words have been used in association with, or to fan the flames of, the killing of other human beings. You know what these words are. These are the words shouted, hissed, or even whispered during the execution of other people. Throughout the ages we have placed people in the center of mobs, and either hung, stoned, or burned them. Words that mobs use to describe their victims should all be on our "words of death" list. I'm sure you can think of some right now. Write them on your danger phrase list, and label them as "words of death." I choose not to repeat them— even here. You know what they are.

Don't ever use these words again.

If you have determined that words have helped contribute to the death and suffering of other human beings, you should take great care to avoid them at all costs. There is power in using the same line that the great Reese Witherspoon immortalized in the timeless classic, "Legally Blonde."

"I don't use that word."

Simple, right? You should have some words and phrases in that category. You'll find great power in being able to say, "I don't use that word" and mean it. Not in private, not in jokes, not ever.

Ever.

Slayer Principle:

Slayers don't use words of death.

What I would like you to do until our next lesson is this: Look around your office, your home, television, radio, wherever people communicate, and pay attention to the phrases that work and the phrases that don't. Start your list of danger phrases and power phrases, and come up with at least ten for each side of your list. Look for moments to purge danger phrases, and use new power phrases instead. Study the verbal patterns of powerful communicators, and ineffective communicators alike. Remember that every person is your assignment, and your master teacher.

Good luck. Until our next lesson....

Homework:

- Keep your Personal Compass handy, and continue updating and tweaking it
- Look for, and write down, at least ten danger phrases
- Look for, and write down, at least ten power phrases on page 9 of the ENERGY VAMPIRE SLAYING: 101 WORKBOOK.
- When you write down your power phrases, say them out loud ten times each.
- Practice using your new danger phrases with other people, at least three times each.
- Use the broken record at least twice.
- Look for the rewards that you are giving the difficult people in your life that actually encourage their difficult behavior.
- Choose a new *Slayer Principles* card and carry it around with you for 24 hours. Pull it out and read it out loud at it at least 5 times throughout the day.

Again, you must do all the above in preparation for your next lesson. You might want to read ahead, and that's OK. If you do read ahead, however, after you put this book down, you must come back to it starting at chapter 6, having done the homework listed above.

You must really be dedicated to have come this far, and because you have done so, I have faith that you will go all the way. Just remember, it takes patience and dedication to reach your full Slayer potential. Take this, and every lesson, seriously, and you will see unbelievable results. Remember also, you have a purpose, and don't let anyone or anything distract you from your purpose (which should be stated in your Personal Compass.)

For the resources that go with this and other chapters, including audio recordings and quick-reference cards, go to http://powerdiversity.com/the-library

Chapter 6: Energy Vampires--name them, know them, slay them

Assuming you have completed all the lessons up to this point, you're now ready to learn some basic slaying maneuvers. You'll be introduced to 10 Energy Vampires in this chapter, and you'll learn their names. It is important to know their names, because once you do, ***the veil will be lifted.***

We come in contact with difficult people, Energy Vampires, and The Negaddicteds all the time, but we get caught up in illusions. When Mr. Jones screams and yells at us, we think his name is still Mr. Jones. The truth is, however, that when this happens, Mr. Jones has left the building, and his body has been taken over by the Exploder EV.

Knowing this, you now have a real Slayer's chance.

You have a chance, because of training like this. Being able to identify the various EVs is key. Knowing who they are, what they want, and how to treat them is unique knowledge that few possess. As a Slayer, it's required learning.

Remember that being a Slayer is not about jamming wooden steaks into people's hearts, or chopping their heads off. Our target is not *destruction*, but instead, ***transformation***. Instead of weapons, we use the knowledge we have of people, and the rewards they seek, to banish the *energy* and its negative vibration. Slayers don't destroy people--they transform people and situations. Once you truly understand that Slayers are transformers, you can use the following tactics to eliminate the effect that EV's have on your life, and you can transform the world around you by seeing it differently. That may sound like quite a hefty claim, but remember, this is just the 101 level course.

That said, you are about to take a gigantic leap in your interpersonal skills, so you might want to get something to drink, make sure you have something to take notes with, and get comfortable.

This lesson might take you several days to complete, and that's OK. Don't rush things. Think about crime shows like Cops and CSI where you see people studying what looks like the family tree of various high-profile crime rings. They have the same photos of the same people up on their offices all the time. Walk into any federal building and you'll see photos of the ten most wanted. The same photos are all over FBI office walls. Why do they all do this? Because the more you study someone--study who they are and what they "look" like--the odds of spotting them, and eventually catching them, increase. It's the same thing with a Slayer looking to identify and handle Energy Vampires.

Pay special attention to the rewards EVs are looking for and remember that when all else fails, and you are wearing down--YOU STILL MUST NOT GIVE THEM THEIR REWARDS. Rewards might shut them up temporarily, but in the long run they are the encouragement that drives the behavior of Energy Vampires. Don't encourage their behavior; shut it down.

Most of us are like walking ATM's (automated teller machines). EV's come up to us, push our buttons, and then stand back and wait for their payout. (Children dealing with their parents are skilled at this as well—almost all children.)Then what do most of us do? We give them just what they're looking for--their payout, or reward. Some of us, however, have learned that if we do not give the payout, or reward, that the EV is looking for, they will leave us alone, and find some other ATM. I mean, would you keep going to an ATM if you knew it never gave you any money? Of course not. Think of this as basically the same thing. If you want the behavior to continue reward it--if you have children you know what I mean. If you want behavior to continue, reward it. If you want behavior to stop, don't reward it —ever.

Do not be the walking ATM the EV is looking for.

The following is the list of the top ten Energy Vampires that you must begin to spot, name, and deal with—starting today.

1. The Exploder
2. The Cry-Baby
3. The Gossip
4. The Negaddicted
5. The Sniper
6. The Time-Sucker
7. The Tank
8. The Beggar
9. The Victim
10. The Bully

OK, let's get started.

THE EXPLODER

Quick Reference Card: #8

How to recognize them: Exploders yell, swear, threaten, insult, and wave their hands in the air. Extreme Exploders have been known to foam at the mouth as their eyes bulge out of their heads (though this is only in the movies).

Who they are: Exploders have lost all self control and are totally in the right (emotional) hemisphere of their brain. They think no one has heard their message, they have been egregiously wronged, and they are operating on pure emotion and chemical rushes from the brain. Exploders, while exploding, are experiencing temporary insanity.

What their rewards are: Exploders are first and foremost looking to engage you. They feel bad and out-of-control, and they want you to feel bad and out-of-control as well. They are also looking for you to give them any excuse to take their explosion to a nuclear level. Exploders are looking for a dramatic reaction to their dramatic behavior.

How to treat them: Listen to, and speak to the emotional (right) side of their brain before speaking to the logical side of their brain. Match their emotional level with a different emotion. Validate their emotional state. This does not mean to admit fault, blame, or to say they are "right." Let them know that you recognize this is serious, and you hear them. This, of course, requires you to put your ego aside and focus on the goal, which should be to move forward. Remember that how they communicate is about them; how you communicate is about you even when you're communicating with an Exploder. Refer to your Personal Compass and *be* the person you decided to *be* before the Exploder came along.

What to do:
1) *POSITION YOURSELF*: If in person, open your eyes wide enough to show your entire iris, and tilt your head to the side. This will show you are alert and engaged, but not aggressive.
2) *VALIDATE*: Speak to their emotion. Use validating power phrases, such as, "Oh, that's horrible," and, "I can see you are really upset," and "I can understand why that would upset you."
3) *COMPLIMENT*: Compliment them on their self control using a phrase such as, "I'm surprised you're not even more upset." This is a particularly effective tactic. People tend to immediately exhibit behavior you compliment them on.
4) *AGREE*: To get *un-stuck*. Exploders need to hear a sentence that begins with, "You're right..." so do just that. This does not mean admitting fault, or validating their behavior. It simply means using a sentence with, "You're right." Try power phrases such as, "You're right this is a problem." Or, "You're right, someone needs to look into this right away." Or, "You're right, this is very frustrating."
5) *TRANSITION WITH PERMISSION*: Once you've validated their emotions, it is time to move forward, but Exploders have very fragile egos, and need to *decide for themselves* when it's time to transition. Try a phrase such as, "Well I can see you're upset, but you're in luck, you've found the right person, and if you can just give me a chance, I think I can help you with this...would that be all right with you?"

What not to do: Don't engage or challenge them; don't take the bait. That is a reward for them, and only encourages the difficult behavior. A true Slayer puts ego aside, and seeks swift resolution. Don't try to prove that you can out-explode them. Why would you want to do that anyway? Don't try to teach them lessons; it is *you* who should be learning the lesson from *them*. Don't stone-wall them. Speak logically right away before addressing emotion. Don't say, "Calm down." Don't say, "You need..." Don't say, "I understand how you feel," (which is different from the power phrase "I understand why that would upset you"—a phrase which you *should* use.

Slayer Principle:

People treat you *the way you allow them* to treat you.

BONUS TACTIC:
If the Exploder you're dealing with is your boss, say this:
"(Name), I **do** want to hear everything you have to say, but **not** like this," and implement the broken record (repeat the same thing over and over).

SAY THIS:

POWER PHRASES:
"Oh that's horrible."
"You're in Luck."
"You've found the right person!"
"I can see you're upset"
"You're right!"
"If you can just give me a chance…"

NOT THIS:

DANGER PHRASES:
"Calm down."
"You need..."
"I understand how you feel."

Special note:

In this example, I am referring to customers and occasional Exploders. If you have a chronic Exploder in your life, remember that you *must* be doing something to encourage that chronic behavior. If an Exploder crosses the line into an **abuser**, this is an entirely different scenario, to be discussed in a different book. If you need further help, or have questions about dealing with your Exploder, please go to the HELP ME DAN section of our website at www.powerdiversity.com.

THE CRY-BABY

Quick Reference Card: #9

How to recognize them: Cry-Babies are easy to spot; they're the ones who cry. All the time. For reasons other than why you and I might cry. They cry to get attention, they cry to avoid communication, they cry to avoid or distract from confrontation, and they cry to avoid taking responsibility. Basically, crying is their defense mechanism. They use it in a multitude of situations.

Who they are: Cry-Babies are *passive-aggressive* communicators, and they generally have low self-esteem. They have learned that most people don't know how to deal with Cry-Babies, so they use crying to throw people off, stall, and distract from whatever issue they would otherwise have to confront. To be clear: Some people are very sensitive, and genuinely cry often out of overwhelming emotion--this is not the Cry-Baby--this is a sensitive person, and it is your job as a Slayer to be patient and more sensitive with them.

What their rewards are: Cry-Babies are looking to distract you--distract you from the issue, distract you from the truth, distract you from someone else, or distract you from their wrong-doings. They are counting on diverting you from focusing on the original message, to focusing on them and their wounds.

How to treat them: Stay on message. Stay on message. Stay on message. Under normal circumstances, if someone is emotionally out of control, I'd tell you to speak to that emotion. In this case, because the emotion tends to be fabricated and deceptive, whatever you do, don't connect, empathize, or get hooked in any way. Disconnection is the key.

What to do: (In this case, I'm going to assume that you and the Cry-Baby are sitting down at a table and the Cry-Baby begins to cry because you confront him or her on an issue.)
   1) **HAVE YOUR TOOLS AT HAND:** Place a box of tissues, and a bottle of water within easy reach.
   2) **DO NOT MAKE PHYSICAL CONTACT:** Cry-Babies are accustomed to people touching them, which further reinforces the connection they're looking for. You want to demonstrate that you are not connecting with them.
   3) **GIVE THEM THE FRONT-TILT AND WIDE-EYES:** Make sure to tilt (and occasionally nod) your head slightly forward and keep your eyes a little more open than you would normally do while you speak. This signals aggression, and lets them know you are not "softening" because of their crying.
   4) **ASK A CLOSED-ENDED QUESTION:** Make it clear that you are going to stay on message by saying something such as, "I can see you're having trouble. Would you like a few seconds to compose yourself, or are you ready to continue now?" As you ask that question--
   5) **MAKE THE OFFERING:** Place the bottle of water in front of the crier, and hand them a tissue.
   6) If they keep crying, use **THE BROKEN RECORD**: Keep repeating the same closed-ended question you originally used--over and over again. Most will compose themselves, if they do need a moment, and will respond with something such as, "Yes, if you could just give me time--this is very difficult for me...you don't understand...." Be very specific and in control with your follow-up phrase, saying something such as, "All right would one minute be enough for you, or do you need two?" Lock them down, and let them know that this conversation is going to happen, and it's going to happen now.

What not to do: Don't empathize, connect, or hook up in any way. Do not engage the Cry-Baby or become involved in the drama such a person thrives on. Don't touch this person in a comforting way, because this will just reward his/her behavior. Avoid making any personal emotional connection. Of course in most communication situations I recommend empathy. In this case you should do just the opposite--*do not connect with them*.

Slayer Principle:

EVs expect a certain result from their behavior--give them something other than what they're expecting, and it throws them off course.

SAY THIS:

POWER PHRASES: "Do you need a minute or two to compose yourself?"
"Are you ready now?"
"I can see you're upset, however..."
"You may be upset, but..."
"Please take a tissue and have a drink of water"

NOT THIS:

DANGER PHRASES: "What's wrong?"
"Don't cry."
"Why are you so upset?"
"Tell me about...(anything)"
"Oh, that's horrible..."
"What can I do to help?"

Special Note:

Make sure to be prepared for your "special meeting" with Cry-Babies. If they sit down with you and start to cry, and you place the bottle of water in front of them, while you simultaneously hand them a tissue and say, "I can see you're having trouble--would you like a few seconds to compose yourself, or are you ready to continue now?" they will immediately become aware that they are dealing with a savvy communicator (i.e. Energy Vampire Slayer) who knows how to stay in control of the conversation. With any luck, the Cry-Baby will stop the show right then and there.

THE GOSSIP

Quick Reference Card: #10

How to recognize them: This one's *easy* to recognize. Gossips talk about anyone who's not in the room. They love to be the first ones to deliver the dirt on their "friends" and coworkers.

Who they are: Gossips are some of the most passive-aggressive communicators. Passive-aggressive *basically* means that people intentionally seek to harm you; they just aren't up front about it. There are many styles of--and reasons for--passive-aggressive communication. Gossips get a feeling of power and feed their egos by being the ones with (what they see as) the most *valuable* information. Generally, they have trouble in their personal and professional relationships because of this character trait.

What their rewards are: Gossips are basically looking for three things. They're looking to 1) gather information *from* you, or 2) deliver information *to* you to achieve the ultimate reward of 3) bonding *with* you. Like it or not, when two people share a secret--or any type of privileged information--a bond is formed.

How to treat them: The first time someone gossips with you, *that's about them.* The 25th time someone gossips with you, ***that's about you***. If you have *chronic* gossipers in your life, it's because you're **participating** in the gossip, which might mean you're simply listening. **YOU** might think that you're working, and trying to tend to your own business, but if they're talking around you and you're not being assertive and stopping the gossip, ***you're participating as much as if you were gossiping yourself***. The difficult part of stopping the Gossip isn't what to say; *that's easy.* It's simply *making the decision* to take yourself out of that loop, and suffer the office-politics and social consequences. While you're gathering the emotional strength to confront the Gossip in your life and declare, "ENOUGH ALREADY!" remember that those who gossip with you will have no qualms about gossiping about you.

I'm assuming that if you're a Potential Slayer reading this book, you're making many of these difficult but positive, life-changing decisions lately. Way to go. That said, you must be very clear and direct when you choose to stop the Gossip. Don't wing it. Practice telling people that when they engage in gossip you'll call them on it. The right closing question will allow people to get themselves off the hook, and will make your confrontation quick, clean, and easy.

What to do:

Give them an **I-C-R**:
I-introduced
C-criticized
R-revealed

And prepare a good **closed-ended closing line**, such as, "Was that your intent?"

Here's how it sounds: "Mary, you just **introduced** Lawanda into our conversation, **criticized** her personally, and **revealed** some pretty sensitive information about her to me, *was that your intent?*"
Most Gossips at this point will giggle uncomfortably and stop. If they don't, tell them, "Again, I am only comfortable talking about people who are present. Now, would you like to go get Lawanda or shall I?"

What not to do: Don't just blindside people without putting them on notice that you're an anti-Gossip Slayer. If it's a problem that's been going on for awhile, don't just one day pull an I-C-R. Let people know that you're changing your ways, by saying something such as, "I know that I may sometimes engage in gossip, but it's a character flaw I'm working on eliminating.

Slayer Principle:

Those who gossip *with* you gossip *about* you.

<u>SAY THIS:</u>

POWER PHRASE: "I am only comfortable talking about people who are present."

And if the Gossip persists,

<u>SAY THIS:</u>

POWER PHRASE: "Would you like to go get Lawanda, or shall I?"

<u>NOT THIS:</u>

DANGER PHRASES: "Why don't you just shut up?"
"You're such a Gossip."
"Tell me more."
"I'm going to tell Lawanda you said that."

Special note:

Follow-through is key. It's so important, I'll say it three more times. Follow-through is key. Follow-through is key. Follow-through is key. You must be assertive, direct, and consistent when communicating with Gossips. If you have them, you trained them to gossip with you, and it's much harder, *but much more rewarding*, to train them to stop.

The Negaddicted

Quick Reference Card: #11

How to recognize them: Look for the dark cloud looming above their heads--the cloud that follows them around wherever they go. They always have criticisms, and rarely have solutions. If they do offer a comment veiled as a solution, it frequently involves destruction rather than creation. They can be either extroverted or introverted, but their mere energy in a room is so toxic it creates a bad taste in your mouth. When these people enter a room, the whole energy changes, and the non-toxic people present become uncomfortable until the Negaddicteds leave. In extreme cases, their faces even have permanent frown lines that only a visit to a dermatologist or med-spa can correct. They definitely do NOT comply with the 5 positives to every 1 negative rule. They are called *toxic* for a reason: Whether in a home or an office, they poison the environment and can make people emotionally, spiritually, and physically sick.

Who they are: Negaddicteds are the saddest people of all. They live in a dark, ugly, place where everything is a total drag, and they want to **drag you** into that world. Forgive them; they just don't know any other way to be. Negativity is part of their *identity*. They are spiraling down a vortex of toxicity because they are entrenched in a pattern of destruction (of their own making, for the most part) and don't know how to change it.

What their rewards are: Negaddicteds are looking for validation and connection. They want you to wallow around with them in the toxic cosmic sludge. They want you to join their downer-party, agree with them, support them, or **if nothing else**, just listen to them.

How to treat them: Redirect. Redirect. Redirect. Let them know clearly that you are on a mission to shine light and positive energy into the world, and you need their help to do it. Surprisingly, Negaddicteds like to feel needed *without having to really do anything.* Later, when they start to say negative things, you can immediately launch into the anti-negativity mode that you set them up for. Remember to put up your shield of white light when you are around a Negaddicted, and make sure to feed your brain something positive before your encounter with them.

What to do:
   1) LAY THE GROUNDWORK by saying something such as, "I need your help. I'm trying to be more positive and avoid negativity. This is very important to me, and will actually help you too because I think you'll enjoy being around me more. If you see me saying or doing anything negative, please point it out, OK?"
   2) Once you've done this, when they start to exhibit their negativity, **SHOOT POSITIVE POWER PHRASES** at them that deflect the negativity without being aggressive.
   3) SUGGEST ALTERNATIVE VIEWPOINTS: Suggest an alternative positive way of looking at things.
   4) ASK THEM what they would do that would make things better.
   5) BE CONSISTENT in your negativity-deflection and assertive communication and they will NOT think talking to you is fun. They will go find their next victim down the hallway.
   6) If all else fails, **RUN AS FAST AS YOU CAN**. In other words, begin to avoid this person for your own mental health.

What not to do: As a Potential Slayer, you must understand that Energy Vampires by definition are miserable. There is never a need, or excuse to add to someone's misery. Do not, however, in any way engage them or respond to their negativity with anything other than well thought-out power phrases. Never agree with them or lead them to believe you are on their team. Stop rewarding the behavior.

Slayer principle:

**You can't shine bright light without charging your own batteries.
Feed your body, mind, and spirit with things that nourish them.**

<u>*SAY THIS:*</u>

POWER PHRASES: "I'm really trying to keep things positive--it's for my health--can you help me do that, please?"
"I really like..."
"What do you think would make it better?"
"Watch--you'll love it" (coupled with the broken record)
"Maybe you should talk to someone about that."
"What solutions do you think would work?"
"Be careful--what you focus on grows, and I'd hate to see *this* grow--for *your* sake"

<u>*NOT THIS:*</u>

DANGER PHRASES: "Oh, that's too bad."
"I agree." (When you really don't…)
"Is there anything I can do?"
"You're right."
"You're so negative."
"What's your problem?"
"What's wrong with you?"
"Will you marry me?" **Avoid this one at all costs!**

Special note:

Negaddicteds, while passive, are among the most dangerous of all EVs. Their energy is poisonous, and can spread like a cancer through an office, or a home. They are a like a cosmic disease, and just like any other disease, they need to be eradicated, or at least *quarantined* in an office setting. Make sure they have little or no contact with those who are still healthy. It's worth it. Negativity destroys productivity. I find that in most organizations, a company-wide training program is needed to remedy the problem. The training must start with management, and every single person should attend. If you're like most people who work in an office these days, you know what I mean. If you need immediate help, call the Slayer Hotline at 877-570-1573, or email us at help@powerdiversity.com.

BONUS TACTIC:

"THE CLICKER"

Every employee in your organization should be issued a clicker—like the ones used for dog training, and be required to carry it at all times. They're cheap, and about the size of a matchbox. When anyone hears something negative, it becomes the obligation of the listener to click the dog clicker (they're super loud) until the offender gets the idea and stops the negative chatter. It gets very annoying for Negaddicteds when everyone is always pointing and clicking at them. It's loud and startling; they WILL break the pattern. Try it. It works, and it's fun for everyone.

THE SNIPER

Quick Reference Card: #12

How to recognize them: Snipers hurl insults masked as humor, and they love to do it in a public forum. When you are in private with Snipers, they might take an occasional pot-shot or two, but nothing like when there's a crowd, or *audience*. They are passive-aggressive communicators in the sense that they like to say insulting things, but they aren't up-front about it.

Who they are: Snipers have relatively high self-esteem, are very ego-driven, and are rarely passive. When Snipers snipe you, it's generally not a big deal to them; they don't plan it out, and they often don't mean much by it. Snipers frequently are just looking for a laugh, or to connect with a group, and they've been trained that this behavior works for them. It's who they are; when they snipe you, it's ***not about you***. How you respond to them, however is ***all about you***. You can't change a Sniper any more than you can change anyone else, but you **must** *train* the Sniper *how to treat you*.

What their rewards are: Snipers are looking for a laugh at your expense with no immediate, personal price to pay. They also enjoy a good verbal spar. They love it when people snipe back--this only adds to the booty, especially if there's a good-sized crowd. They are assuming no one is going to call them on their behavior because people almost never do.

How to treat them: Call them on their behavior. Be calm, direct, and assertive, but not aggressive, because 1) they like to make you angry—it's a reward for them, and 2) *a calm direct and assertive person is who you strive to be anyway—right?* Everything from your body language to your words needs to be direct, clear, non-retaliatory, and assertive. When sniped, we have a tendency to react, and want to snipe back, and get the last burn. Don't do that. Instead, remember your Personal Compass.

What to do: Give them the *Sniper 4-Step*
>**1) GET INTO POSITION:** Face them dead-on physically, make direct eye contact, and tilt your head slightly forward. DO NOT let your head tilt to the side.
>**2) CALL THEM BY NAME:** Say their first name.
>**3) BACKTRACK:** Repeat back to them what they just said--word-for-word if you can.
>**4) ASK A SPOTLIGHT QUESTION:** A spotlight question is a question that shines light on the person to whom you say it, thus bringing the situation to light. Spotlight questions always have the same lead-in-line, which is, "Are you trying to...?"

To put it all together, let's say you're standing in the hallway, and you just came from a meeting. You presented an idea to the board. The Sniper thought you bombed, but didn't help you at the time, or say anything until now, when she is surrounded by her friends, and you are all alone. As you pass the group in the hallway, the Sniper says to you, "Hey Gonzalez--I forgot to congratulate you on a spectacular presentation in front of the board. You really looked intelligent. Way to go!"

She smiles like a snake as she says it. People in the group either laugh, smile or look awkward. You, however, have prepared, and respond by turning to face the Sniper completely, looking her in the eyes, tilting your head forward, and saying, "Shaniqua, you just said, "Hey Gonzalez--I forgot to congratulate you on a spectacular presentation in front of the board yesterday. You really looked intelligent. Way to go." Are you trying to insult me?"

At this point the Sniper normally responds with a "Sheesh, I was just joking...don't take it so seriously." To which you respond with The Three Second Look, and calmly walk away.

Of course, sometimes the Sniper says, "Oh, let me be more direct. You looked like a moron." This happens far less frequently, but it does happen, which is why you need as many tactics as possible with which to respond. You'll find more tactics in the next chapter, in the quick-reference cards in the back of this book, and on our website. The more tactics you have, the more you can stand your ground and slay the EV without ever *becoming* an EV.

BONUS TACTIC--The Three-Second-Look:

You use the Three-Second-Look when someone wants you to verbally respond to them. Instead of responding, you simply stare them in the eyes without smiling, for the count of three (three looooong seconds). This is hard-wired, built-in, *instinctive* assertive, or "*alpha-dog*" behavior. (**Fun Fact:** When held for seven seconds or more, eye contact becomes very aggressive, and actually causes a chemical reaction in our brain.) Under normal circumstances, the savvy communicator breaks the eye contact, even if just for a split-second, at least every 7 seconds.

The Sniper will now think, "Yeeesh, that wasn't fun like it normally is," and they will choose a different victim *the next time*. Again, **consistency** is the key, and especially with Snipers who are very ego-driven. It sometimes takes several attempts to train Snipers that they will not find their rewards *with you*.

What not to do: Under no circumstances are you to engage in a battle of wits with the Sniper. That's *fun* for them. It only makes them come back to you again and again. Don't *ever* wing it. **EVER.** Don't say the first thing into your brain when you're sniped, because it's as if you're in shock. Like it or not, when sniped, the brain releases chemicals, the flight-or-fight instinct kicks in, and you aren't thinking clearly. Show **no** signs of weakness or you run the risk of being a constant source of amusement for them. Don't just ignore the behavior, either. A Sniper needs to know that you will respond to them, but not as they're used to. You will be assertive, and force them to be up-front with their communication, but you will not engage in unenlightened, unprofessional, or aggressive behavior Slayers don't do that.

Slayer Principle:

You can't change people, but you can *train them how to treat you*.

<u>**SAY THIS:**</u>

POWER PHRASES:
"Are you trying to..."
"Why would you say that?"
"Why would you ask that?"
"Ooh, that hurt."
"I don't communicate like that, and I'd appreciate it if you didn't communicate like that with me."
"I invite criticism; I just ask you to be direct about it."

<u>**NOT THIS:**</u>

DANGER PHRASES:
"You're an idiot."
"That's not nice."
"Oh yeah, well..."
"I don't appreciate..."

Special Note:

If after a few attempts at using the Sniper 4-Step, you're not getting the results you're looking for, don't get discouraged. Snipers are sometimes very persistent. They can't help it--they are ego-driven creatures. Forgive them for that. With the Sniper, as with any difficult person, if at first you don't succeed, try another tactic. You'll find tactics and scripts that you can try in a variety of different situations in the quick-reference flash-card section of this program. Choose a different card each week to focus on, and keep trying new tactics until you find one that works for you. Trust me, as The Energy Vampire Slayer, I can tell you that there is ***always*** something that will work.

THE TIME-SUCKER

Quick Reference Card: #13

How to recognize them: They're the ones who come into your space and have no regard for whatever it is you're doing. They actually *are oblivious* to the fact that you are serious about your work, and don't just goof off all the time, as they do. They just come in and start speaking. Many times they'll start the conversation with, "I'm bored." Other times they just encourage you to "take a break" because they have nothing to do at the moment.

Who they are: They mean no harm, so there is no need to be aggressive with them, but you must be assertive. They are generally unfocused, and not conscious or respectful of time. Furthermore, they frequently arrive late to work, and leave early.

What their rewards are: They're generally looking for a distraction, a confidant, or a playmate. They could, however actually be seeking help or advice, and are simply unaware of proper etiquette and boundaries. The bottom line is *they want your time*.

How to treat them: You must be extremely assertive with Time-Suckers, set very clear boundaries, and give them very clear instructions. You must train them to understand how you spend our time, and what your boundaries are. You must first explain verbally what the rules are, and if that doesn't work, use a business tool. A great business tool for combating Time-Suckers is a little sign called an Availability Monitor that you can make out of construction paper. It looks like this:

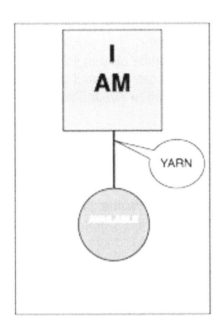 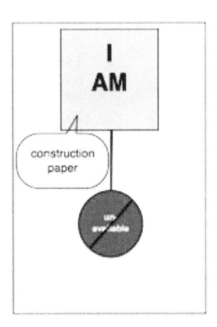

Just use red construction paper on one side of the circle, and green on the other, then flip it to the appropriate color during the day. Of course, it is up to you to be vigilant and make sure your monitor is updated and accurate. When the Time-Sucker comes into your space uninvited, all you have to do, without stopping what you're doing, without saying a word--is point to the sign. (You can use an object such as a pen to point, or you can use your finger, provided you don't use the middle finger....)

What to do:

1) MAKE AN AVAILABILITY MONITOR

2) SCRIPT OUT A TALK. You can use a D-E-S-C script, found in the quick- reference cards in the back of this book, and also on our website in the customer resources section. It would sound something like this:

Lead-in Line: "Trixie, I need your help."

D: "I'm really trying to stay focused, and to stop getting distracted when I'm at work."

E: "When I get distracted, it is more difficult for me to go back to what I was doing, and it really hurts my production, and frustrates me."

S: "If you could help me by checking my Availability Monitor, and if it's green, meaning *available*, go ahead and grab my attention, that would be great. If it's red, meaning *unavailable*, unless it's an extreme emergency, please shoot me an email telling me what you need, and as soon as I'm available, I'll get right back to you."

C: "That way, you will be able to have my full attention when we *do* talk."

Closing Line: "Can I count on you do to that?"

(The D-E-S-C script is explained on our website in the Professional Communication podcast series, and also at the end of this book in the quick-reference card section.)

3) USE YOUR AVAILABILITY MONITOR, and be consistent. Let the Time-Sucker see that you use it all the time, with everyone. You might even consider making a bunch of them, and passing them out as gifts. Trust me--everyone will love them.

What not to do: This one is pretty simple: The first time Time-Suckers get away with sucking time from you, that's about them. The 17th time—that's about you. Set boundaries as described above, and stick to your guns. This one *is all about you*. Don't allow someone to steal your time just because you feel uncomfortable being assertive. Assertive skills are learned, and the more you practice, the easier it becomes to protect your time, and your other valuable resources.

Slayer Principle:
Time is the coin of your life. It is the only coin you have, and only you can determine how it will be spent. Be careful lest you let other people spend it for you.

Carl Sandburg
US Biographer & Poet (1878 - 1967)

<u>**SAY THIS:**</u>

POWER PHRASES: "I need your help"
"I'm really trying to stay focused and stop getting distracted when I'm at work."
"If you could help me by checking my Availability Monitor..."
"That way, you will be able to have my full attention when we *do* talk"
"Can I count on you to do that?"
"I am right in the middle of something...can you shoot me an email and I'll get back to you?"

<u>**NOT THIS:**</u>

DANGER PHRASES: "Leave me alone"
"Can't you see I'm busy?"
"I just have a minute"
"Can it wait?"
"WHAAAAAT?"

Special Note:
When you are concentrating at work, and you are interrupted, the interruption actually causes a change in your brain waves. When you return to whatever it is you were doing, you are at a diminished capacity compared to where you were before the interruption. You can't just "get right back into" whatever it was you were doing. Your brain needs to ramp-up again. While Time-Suckers seem relatively harmless, they can seriously impact your production at work by stealing your actual time, and delaying you further by causing a disruption to the flow of your work and the functioning of your brain. Their impact is even greater than it appears at the moment.

THE TANK

Quick Reference Card: #14

How to recognize them: They're the ones who, instead of losing emotional control, (as Exploders do) *seem* to be totally in control as they roll right over you with their words. They are aggressive communicators when they are in full-out Tank mode, and it's very difficult to interrupt them. They just keep going and going and going and going and going. They are going to keep rolling over you and firing at you with their words until they think they "win." They frequently raise their voice and often use profanity, but they do not scream, yell, and throw wild fits. They are very targeted, direct, and difficult to stop.

Who they are: They are generally very left-brained people, who have been pushed past the limit, and feel as if there's something you *just don't get*. They won't stop until you get it. They are very verbally-skilled, and can keep talking, and charging at you verbally *forever* if they need to. The good news is that they will generally cross the line into verbal abuse, threats, or, as mentioned before--profanity. That's your cue to interrupt and slay the EV within them.

What their rewards are: Tanks are made for battle. The have two clear goals: 1) They want a good verbal war, and 2) they want something specific and **they'll tell you what it is**. They want to win the war, and enjoy the spoils, and they want to think they won the war because they are powerful. Tanks are looking for you to surrender and either agree with them or give them what they want. They will keep firing until they believe they've won the battle.

How to treat them: This one is fairly simple: Let them win. This is simple in the sense that the method is simple. But the difficult part is putting our own egos aside while we do this. The Tanks want to be right; let them be right. The Tanks want you to surrender; let yourself surrender. After all, in your defenselessness your safety lies. (For more on this concept, visit http://www.powerdiversity.com/ podcasts, and listen to the "In My Defenselessness My Safety Lies" audio podcast in our "Something to Think About/Inspirational Thought for the Day" series.

What to do:

    1) INTERRUPT THEM: This is a great tactic you can use all the time. When someone is rolling over you, and you can't get a word in edgewise, say their name loudly and firmly over and over again until they stop and say, "WHAT?!" It is almost impossible for human beings not to stop and respond to their own name. Once they do, you have the floor. Generally saying the name three times will do it—e.g. Bill! **Bill! BILL!**

    2) AGREE WITH THEM: This is a tactic we use with other EVs as well. Keep starting sentences with, "You're right..." and find ways to agree with them, similar to how you learned to agree with the Exploder.

    3) GIVE THEM BOTTOM-LINE STATEMENTS: Bottom-line statements are basically "the rules" for communicating with you. They are statements that tell people what you will and will not put up with. They generally start out with the lead-in line, "I don't allow..."

    4) GIVE THEM BOUNDARY STATEMENTS: Boundary statements clearly let people know that you are willing to communicate with them, but not under these circumstances. A boundary statement for a Tank can sound like this, "I want to hear everything that you have to say, but not in this manner."

    5) USE A RE-DIRECT WITH ASSUMPTIONS: A re-direct with assumptions re-directs someone's behavior in another direction under the assumption that they will change, and you're going to tell them in advance what their reward will be once they do change. The verbal pattern is easy, and sounds like this: "When you're ready to...I'll be ready to..."

6) USE EMPOWERMENT STATEMENTS: Empowerment statements give the person to whom you are speaking options, and a sense of power. Tanks in particular want a sense of power and control, so empowerment statements are great tactics to use with them. "Are you ready now?" Or, "Would you like to discuss this calmly now, or would you like to revisit this later?"

To put it all together, let's say you have a Tank in your office, and they're upset about the raise they didn't get. They've been going on for five minutes, and you've tried to interrupt their rampage to explain to them what the situation is and why they didn't get the raise they expected. As I mentioned earlier, Tanks will almost certainly use profanity, threaten you, or become verbally abusive--that's your cue. It's like a gift they give you that says, "OK Slayer! Here's your chance!"

What you say might sound something like this: "BILL! BILL! BILL! You're right, this is very disappointing, but I don't allow profanity in my office, and though I want to hear everything you have to say, I will not communicate this way. Once you're ready to speak to me in a calm, professional manner, I'll be ready to continue this conversation--but not until then. Do you need a few minutes, or are you ready now?"

Slayer Principle:

In your defenselessness your safety lies.

-Loosely translated from *A Course in Miracles*

SAY THIS:

POWER PHRASES: "Bill! Bill Bill!" (Or whatever his/her name is)
"You're right!"
"I don't allow..."
"I do want to hear everything you have to say, but not in this manner."
"When you're ready to...I'll be ready to..."
"Are you ready now?"

NOT THIS:

DANGER PHRASES: "Excuse me...if I could just say something..."
"Would you please settle down?"
"If you would just listen..."
"You're just plain wrong."
"I'm not going to stand here and listen to this."

Special Note:

Tanks can sometimes be confused with abusers. We have all occasionally said things that can be taken as verbal abuse...that's only human. However, truly abusive people chronically engage in this behavior, and intend to inflict pain with their words or fists. This is totally different from what we are discussing here. The rule with abusers is almost always the same: Walk away--sometimes RUN away. There are many strategies that have been shown to be effective in altering the behavior of Tanks and other EV's. In general, we can train people how to treat us. Having said that...there is no tactic or strategy that has ever been proven to transform abusive people into non-abusive people. Just like cancer, abusive people must be cut out and eradicated from your life—completely.

THE BEGGAR

Quick Reference Card: #15

How to recognize them: They want one of your two most precious resources--your time, or your money—or sometimes both. They could be selling candy bars for their kid's scout troop, or putting a committee together for Sherri's going-away party, or soliciting a contribution for United Way. Or perhaps they're just a little short of cash today and need you to spot them for lunch. (Of course they'll pay you back when they're paid—at the end of the week.) Sure sign you're talking to a Beggar? They won't take *no* for an answer.

Who they are: They have no idea how out-of-line it is to be asking for your time or money in the workplace. They have no idea they are pressuring or embarrassing you, or if they do have this figured out, they proceed ahead, anyway. They are *generally* clueless that they are being inappropriate and pushy.

They frequently think they're doing someone a favor, or if the money is for themselves, they think it's just a little favor--what's the big deal?

What their rewards are: They will tell you exactly what it is they want, hoping to appeal either to your generosity or guilt. They are rewarded by your forking over either the time or money they ask for. This is one of the most simple EVs to slay if you're assertive. If, however, you're more passive by nature, and find it difficult to say *no*, you'll need a plan. (And even if you're assertive, you will want a plan for dealing with Beggars, to assure that your communication with them remains savvy and not rude.) Don't worry--I'll give you the plan.

How to treat them: This Energy Vampire is simple to slay if you practice the 4-step process for saying *no* (described below) and just stick to your guns. Most Beggars have been trained that if they badger enough, most people will give them what they want. It is up to you to train them that you are not going to cave in. If you consistently practice this 4-step *no* with Beggars, they will actually stop asking you, knowing that you're "one of those" who doesn't give them what they want.

What to do: First and foremost, start saying *yes* to yourself. Look at your calendar and to-do lists. Are you on them? I mean have you allocated time for yourself and the things you enjoy doing? If not, put yourself on those lists. That's number one. People have a hard time saying *no* to other people if they never say *yes* to themselves. It sounds strange, but it's the truth. That said, the best way to handle Beggars is to give them the 4-step Diplomatic Decline, and stick to your guns using the Broken Record. This is a simple strategy to learn. It consists of four easy steps, followed by the Broken Record.

1 – Sympathize
2 – Say *no*
3 – Say why
4 – Suggest alternatives
5 – Use the Broken Record

Before I give you an example, let me give you a couple tips: 1)The more you talk, the less credibility and strength you'll project, and 2) use the Broken Record as often as necessary until the listener gets the point. This does two things for you. First it makes your life easier because you don't have to think up new words and ideas to articulate as you go along. And second it sends a really strong message that the Beggar can keep asking until he or she is blue in the face, but your answer will be the same--*no*. Most people, when saying *no*, don't do this. They keep adding new excuses, which only gets them into more trouble until they cave. Or they try to stick to their guns and repeat themselves (repeat what they believe is conveying *no*), but they fail because the words are flying out of their mouth haphazardly. This will not happen to you if you master this tactic. You'll be able to easily repeat yourself nearly word for word if you're using this tactic to frame your response.

Let's talk about each one of the four steps.

Step 1 – Sympathize: This helps soften the *no*. You want to tell the other person that you recognize that this is important to them and you're not discounting their needs right now. "I understand you're in a bind," for example (as opposed to the Danger Phrase "I understand how you feel.") The Power Phrase that I've found particularly effective is: "I can understand what a bind you're in and under normal circumstances…" When you tell someone, "Boy I can understand what a bind you're in, and under normal circumstances I would love to help", the listener assumes these must be extraordinary circumstances and is apt to shelve further arguments.

Step 2 – Say *no*: It's amazing how often people think that they're saying *no* when in fact they never actually say *no*. They say things such as, "Oh I'd love to but I'm a little short on cash right now." This is not a *no*. Or they will say something such as, "I'd love to, but my mom is in town." Again this is not a *no*. These are simply invitations for the other person to tell us how he or she can help make it possible. "Oh I can lend you money for awhile" or "Oh your mom can come too. Wouldn't that be fun?" A great Power Phrase to get the *no* out of your mouth is, "… however, unfortunately I can't." That's a *no*. In this instance, as in many, if you don't have a clear script prepared in advance, what comes out of the mouth tends to be all wrong.

Step 3 – Say why: Again, people tend to ask us for one of two things—our time or our money, and we seem to struggle with these issues every single time. But not any more! Remember: Don't give excuses. Instead, if someone asks you for your time, use the Power Phrase, "I have other plans." Don't say what they are or you're really asking for trouble. The Slayer does not explain any further. Your plans could be that you intend to sit at home alone watching American Idol and shoving a cheese pizza in your face all alone in a dark room. You deserve to be able to keep those plans. If someone asks for your money, try the Power Phrase, "It's not in my budget." Nobody knows what your budget is. You could have a $2500 budget for beer and poker, but that's your budget. Now with these two responses, if you use them, you should be able to answer 99% of requests with an effective *NO* if that's what you want.

Step 4 – Suggest alternatives: There is no specific Power Phrase for this but just remember that you'll have to live with your suggestions. If you tell your boss to ask you again, if this comes up at a later date--be prepared to say *yes* later. If you tell a coworker to go ask Mary, make sure Mary won't come looking for you later. If you say you'll work on the campaign next year, don't forget to say *yes* when next year comes around. Find an alternative you can live with--there always is one if you're clever, and if you're reading this--you're clever.

Step 5-Use the broken record: Beggars count on your changing your story, and they use that, and your new excuses, to wear you down and get you to a *yes*. (Children are wonderful examples of how successful Beggars can be at wearing people down.) DON'T LET ANYONE WEAR YOU DOWN and don't change your story and add to it! The words you said the first time will suffice. Say them again and again until the point is made. This method is more effective, and far less stressful for you as opposed to thinking up excuses.

Let's put it all together. It would sound something like this. "Hey, you know we're throwing a party for Susie in accounting who's leaving the company. Everyone's pitching in $10 to buy her a big going away present. Can I count on you?" Here's how the *no* sounds using the 4-Step Diplomatic Decline. "Boy Mary, that sounds like a great idea, and under normal circumstances I might. However, unfortunately I can't because I'm on a strict budget and that's just not in it. But ask me if something like this comes up again in about six months and I'll see if I can fit it into my budget." "Ahh, how about just $5?" "Again, Mary unfortunately I can't because I'm on a strict budget and that's just not in it but ask me if something like this comes up again in about six months and I'll see if I can fit it into my budget." "Please just a couple of bucks." "Again, Mary unfortunately I can't because I'm on a strict budget and that's not in it but ask me again if something like this comes up again in six months and I will see if I can fit it into my budget." How long do you think that would continue? The moment that you say something different you have to start back at square one. What's interesting about the Broken Record is that when people hear you say *no* they might ignore it the first time. When they push it and you give them *no* the second time, they may still have hope. But when you say *no* the third time, people tend to recognize that you're going to keep saying the same thing over and over, and you mean it. You'll have trained them that your *no* means *no*. Let's try again with the boss who wants you to work late.

"Hey, Charlie you know I'm really in a bind and I need someone to stay after work tonight for a few hours and I'm really counting on you. So what do you say?" "Oh, you know Mr. Jones, I know that you must really be in a bind and under normal circumstances I would, however unfortunately I can't because I've made other plans and I simply can't break them. But maybe I could come in early tomorrow. Would that work for you?" "Oh, no I really need that done tonight. Can't you stay just this one time? I'm really counting on you. "Boy I know you must really be in a bind to ask me like this and under normal circumstances I would, however unfortunately I can't because I've made other plans I simply can't break, but maybe I could come in early tomorrow. Would that work for you?" The boss says, "What are you doing?" And you could reply, "Well that's interesting, why would you ask." He responds, "Because I'm really in a bind." Now you reiterate, "I can really appreciate that, and again, under normal circumstances I would, however tonight unfortunately I can't." Now how long do you think that would go on? Using this technique helps you say *no* so that people hear it. It softens it so that there is no offense given, yet your use of the technique shows people that you aren't like most other communicators—namely ineffective. You're different, and your *no* means *no*.

Slayer Principle:

It's much easier to say *no* to other people when you first say *yes* to yourself.

<u>SAY THIS:</u>

POWER PHRASES: "Under Normal Circumstances…"
"Unfortunately I can't"
"I have other plans."
"It's not in my budget."
"I simply can't."
"Because, I just can't."

<u>NOT THIS:</u>

DANGER PHRASES: "I'm sorry."
"I understand how you feel."
"I'd like to."
"Let me think about it."
"No."

Special Note:

When you decide to say *no* to the Beggar, you must realize there is a price to pay. This is a cost-benefit situation. If you're the one who says *no* most often, you will most likely be "labeled," and people might think of you as miserly with your time, money, or whatever. Only you can decide if it's worth it for you. We all give to Beggars at times, and sometimes it's appropriate, but it should be something that you do because you *want* to, not because you feel intimidated. If you choose to say *no*, use the tactic above, and your problems will be solved. The tactic is easy to learn--it's making the decision to say *no* to a Beggar that's difficult--the choice is yours.

THE VICTIM

Quick Reference Card: #16

How to recognize them: They put on Academy Award-Winning performances as they tell you about their latest tragedy, their day-to-day struggles, and how they keep getting victimized for no reason. It's never their fault, and there's always *something* dramatic going on in their lives. If there's no series of unfortunate events befalling them at the moment, they've been known to fabricate (or *invent*) stories out of whole cloth. It's important to keep in mind that while they're telling their stories, *THEY AREN'T REALLY LYING* even if the stories aren't entirely true. They actually **believe** the stories they tell (from their perspective, of course) and they see the world as against them.

Who they are: Victims are generally very passive, or passive-aggressive communicators, and slightly (or completely) out of touch with reality. They are not in charge of their lives, and need leadership and guidance, along with constant instruction and supervision. Despite all this help, however, Victims frequently self-sabotage. They don't mean to be complainers or melodramatic; they have simply been in a Victim-mentality cycle, and they can't see clearly.

What their rewards are: Victims are looking for you to listen to their stories, believe them, validate them, and sympathize with them. They also want to bond with you and drag you into their Psycho horror-movie of a life. They tend to be clingy, and love it when they can cling to *you*.

How to treat them: Victims are actually one of the most helpful EVs to Potential Slayers because you can practice your skills with them, and they make it easy for you to do so. As I said earlier, they make *great followers*--a perfect opportunity for you to practice your leadership and communication skills, and re-train them how to communicate *with you*. You must shine an uber-ray of light on them, and they will either see it, and come to the light, or they will run away from you because you ruin their pity-party. While it's always sweetest when you can transform an EV, you also win if your actions result in the EV avoiding you. Either way—you win.

What to do:

   1) GIVE THEM A D-E-S-C SCIPT: Script out a talk in which you tell the Victim that you need to change the way the two of you communicate. This part is the hardest for most, so I suggest using a simple **D-E-S-C** script such as the one below to make your communication easier and more effective. DESC stands for **Describe** the problem, state the **Effects**, **Say** what you want, name the **Consequences**—preceded by a lead-in line, and followed by a closing line. For more about scripting, stop by our blog at http://powerdiversity.com/category/dans-communication-blog. I recommend this particular script, because it's quick, easy, and to the point. It would sound something like this:

   Lead-in-line: "Lindsey, I need your help."

   D- "There has been too much talk of lack and negativity lately."
   E- "This really disturbs me because--you know--what you focus on grows, and I don't want tragedy and negativity to grow in my life or in yours."
   S- "So I'd appreciate it if you can help me with this by telling be about all the good things going on in your life, and we can focus on those. I promise to do the same with you.
   C- "This way, we can focus on--and manifest--more wonderful things in our lives."

   Closing line: "Can I count on you to help me?" (Victims always say *yes*, even if they grimace as they do so. Again, they are passive, and tend to do what they're told, or at least pretend to, while you're watching, and that's good enough with the Victim**.)**

2) GIVE AN EXAMPLE: Now it's time to immediately show how serious you are by talking about positive things. To make it easy, you can use the lead-in-line:

"Speaking of positive things..."

For example: "Speaking of positive things...did you know that Marcia's daughter is going to college this spring? Isn't that wonderful?"

3) USE THE 3-STEP "DITCHING" TECHNIQUE: In the future, every time the Victim starts telling you about the latest drama, use this 3-step process:

a. **USE A "STOP"** gesture, such as putting the palm of your hand up towards the Victim.

b. **USE THE VICTIM'S NAME** to snap them out of it—three times if necessary. For example: "Lindsey! LINDSEY! **LINDSEY!**"

c. **MAKE YOUR EXIT** by saying something such as, "I realize you need to talk about this with someone, but unfortunately, I can't be that person right now." And SCRAM as fast as you can.

Some Victims immediately stop looking to you to validate them, and they find someone else right away. Some Victims take longer. Be consistent with your tactic and it will work. Remember, the first time they told you their sob story that was about them...if the Victim keeps coming back to you, **that's about you.** This technique can seem difficult and even a bit harsh if assertive communication doesn't come easily to you, but after you try it, and see what sweet relief it brings to your life, you'll be amazed at how much easier it becomes to use the technique the next time.

What not to do: Don't challenge Victims, or try and "catch" them in a lie or exaggeration. If you challenge them on their version of the truth, this is also a reward for them because it will give them something to do—namely prove something to you, which will only make them appear to you more frequently. Don't try and make them "fess-up," take responsibility, or see things differently. You can't teach them anything, and besides, you're not there to teach them.

Slayer Principle:

It is not our job to teach Energy Vampires a lesson; it is *their* job to teach *us* a lesson.

In this case, the lesson may be for you to learn how to divest yourself of--and deflect--negativity and the Victim mentality. It's not easy, but if it were, *everyone would be an Energy Vampire Slayer.*

SAY THIS:

POWER PHRASES:
"I'm glad you're not dwelling on it."
"So what lesson did you learn?"
"Thanks for reminding me--I'm going to go write in my Gratitude Journal."
"I admire your tenacity."
"You should talk to someone about that."
"Now that you know, you can break that cycle, huh?"

NOT THIS:

DANGER PHRASES:
"Oh, come on--is it really that bad?"
"Oh, that's horrible."
"Do you want to talk about it?"
"How can I help?"
"No way—you're lying."

Special note:

We are *all* occasional victims. Tragedies *really do* happen, and they happen to us all. We all need a shoulder to cry on sometimes. This is not what we're talking about here. In this case, we're talking about someone who is entrenched in the Victim mentality. If your personality type is that of the lover, or the relator, you might have a tendency to want to help Victims, teach them, and take them under your wing. DON'T DO THAT! (See Slayer Principle above.) The Victim, although seemingly harmless, is a tremendous time-waster and downer. Show Victims how to treat you. They either leave their victimhood at the door, or they go away altogether—their choice.

THE BULLY

Quick Reference Card # 17

How to recognize them: They are the really *mean* ones. Bullies like to **hurt** people. Whether they lash out with their words, actions, or fists, Bullies are out to seek and destroy. They exhibit this behavior in both private and in public settings. Bullies spend most of their time pushing people around physically and verbally, and most people don't push back or retaliate. When they are not in Bully mode, Bullies are generally fun to be with, charismatic, and very endearing--especially to those who like to be saviors, or caretakers--because Bullies by nature tend to be more *broken* than other people.

Who they are: Bullies are extremely aggressive or passive-aggressive. They have deep sacred wounds that have yet to heal, and although it may not appear so on the surface, they are in almost perpetual pain and agony. They may be smart (and even *clever*), but tend not to be terribly intellectual or introspective--

opting instead to focus on the world and people *around* them. Whether consciously or unconsciously, they are in an almost constant state of destruction because it's all they know. They are hurting, and ***HURTING PEOPLE HURT PEOPLE***.

What their rewards are: Bullies are looking for an outlet, or a victim or a challenger. Bullies are an equal-opportunity attacker; you could be their coworker, their lover, their mother, or a total stranger. They generally have a "fix" or *quota* of Bullying they must meet every day, and if they have yet to meet their quota, they will try to victimize and/or destroy just about anything and anyone that has the misfortune of being in their path. *Remember: if you challenge Bullies, and decide to "teach them a lesson" this is also a reward for them.*

How to treat them: The more ego-driven you are, the more you will want to challenge the Bully. This is where many Potentials go wrong--they feel the need to validate their own egos, teach the Bully a lesson, or defend an innocent victim, so they engage a Bully, in a futile attempt to achieve one of these results. **Don't go down this losing road.** First of all, no one else can help you validate your own ego; secondly, people (including Bullies) are here to teach *you* lessons, not the other way around; and finally, if someone truly is being victimized by a Bully and you want to help, the way to do so is to "*deny access*" or prevent contact between the Bully and the victim. Notice this is different from *engaging the Bully*. When you encounter a Bully, your job is to be assertive (not aggressive) without giving him/her the reward of a good fight (which will only encourage them to come back for more).

What to do:
Bullies are by nature very primal and instinctive with their communication style, and are skilled at reading body language, whether they are conscious of this skill or not. In the wild, when a predator is choosing its prey, it is the physical language of the potential prey that signals whether or not it's an easy mark, or if the predator should move on and seek out another target. Once you have established yourself as assertive, and someone who does not offer the rewards they are looking for, or in other words, when you demonstrate that you are not an "easy mark" the bully will find an easier, more suitable target.

The key to dealing with Bullies is two-fold

That said, when confronting an office Bully:

If you feel like you **shouldn't** *verbally* respond, do this:

1) Stand up straight, and face the Bully head-on. Most people turn defensively away from the Bully.

2) Make direct eye contact. Most people dart their eyes away from a Bully, especially when attacked.

3) Don't cross your arms. This signals that you feel you need to defend. The Bully needs to see you on the offense, rather than the defense.

4) Lean in to the Bully with your shoulders back and chest out. This is a very aggressive stance, and signals that you are not an easy target.

5) Keep your head tilted slightly forward, not tilted to the side. When you tilt your head to the side, it sends a passive message--the opposite from the message you want to send.

6) Give the Bully a "Three-Second Look." Stare the Bully in the eyes for three seconds without moving a muscle, then turn and make your exit or go back to working without saying a word. If a Bully takes you off guard, and it's difficult for you to find the words, a three-second look alone is a great tactic for Bullies. It lets them know that you will not engage them, but neither will you back down from them or become a victim.

If you feel you **should** *verbally* respond, say this:

1) Use the Bully's first name.

2) Use spotlight questions that begin with "Are you trying to..."

3) Use bottom-line statements that begin with "I don't..."

4) STAY ON MESSAGE by using the **Broken Record**. Find your core power phrases and stick to them. Start changing your words, and the Bully smells weakness. Stay on message, repeat the same thing over and over, and the Bully will retreat. For example, the Bully might ask you, "Are you done with that project yet?" and it's an obvious "hostile question" to which you respond, "Samantha, I don't answer to you." From that point forward, the most effective thing to do is calmly and confidently repeat the same thing over and over. Don't explain more, don't rationalize, and above all, *don't take the bait.* The only word you're allowed to add is the word because, making the phrase, "***Because Samantha, I don't answer to you.***"

REMEMBER: Always leave, or disengage only after giving the Bully the Three-Second Look.

What not to do: Don't try to *teach the Bully a lesson*, or *prove* anything to the Bully. There is nothing you can teach a Bully other than the fact that you will not make a suitable victim, or target. Our egos can get easily caught up in playing mind-games and trying to win wars against Bullies.

Slayer Principle:

The Slayer knows that the goal is not to win the war, but to instead *rise above the battlefield.*

In this case, the lesson may be for you to learn how to separate yourself from your ego, which sometimes feels challenged, and wants to engage with a Bully. Remember that whatever the ego wants to do is *always the wrong thing to do.* It's not easy to put your ego aside, but if it were, *everyone would be an Energy Vampire Slayer.*

SAY THIS:

POWER PHRASES:	"Are you trying to pick a fight with me?"
	"Interesting, why would you do that?"
	"I don't respond to things like that."
	"I don't communicate that way."
	"I understand what you're saying."
	"This type of communication might be OK with some people, but it's not with me."

NOT THIS:

DANGER PHRASES:	"I'm sorry..."
	"That's not very nice."
	"What's wrong with you?"
	"You're a _____"
	"I don't appreciate..."

Special note:

Of course, we've all experienced many types of Bullies. Some of us get bullied at school, some of us at work, and unfortunately, some of us in our own homes. While this strategy can be used in a variety of different circumstances, it is specifically meant for office Bullies. If you're having trouble with another type of Bully and you don't know what to do, email us right away at help@powerdiversity.com.

What I would like you to do until our next lesson is this: Look around your office, your home, television, radio, wherever people communicate, and pay attention to the phrases that work and the phrases that don't. Start your list of danger phrases and power phrases, and come up with at least ten for each side of your list. Look for moments to purge danger phrases, and use new power phrases instead. Study the verbal patterns of powerful communicators, and ineffective communicators alike. Remember that every person is your assignment, and your master teacher.

Good luck. Until our next lesson.

Homework:
- Keep your Personal Compass handy, and continue updating and tweaking it
- Look for, and write down, at least ten danger phrases
- Look for, and write down, at least ten power phrases
- When you write down your power phrases, say them out loud ten times each
- Practice using your new danger phrases with other people, at least three times each
- Use the broken record at least twice
- Look for the rewards that you are giving the difficult people in your life that actually encourage their difficult behavior
- Complete page 10 in your ENERGY VAMPIRE SLAYING: 101 WORKBOOK where you'll identify your biggest EV, and strategize about how to deal with them.

Again, you must do all the above in preparation for your next lesson. You might want to read ahead, and that's OK. If you do read ahead, however, after you put this book down, you must come back to it starting at chapter 6, having done the homework listed above.

You must really be dedicated to have come this far, and because you have done so, I have faith that you will go all the way. Just remember, it takes patience and dedication to reach your full Slayer potential. Take this, and every lesson, seriously, and you will see unbelievable results. Remember also, you have a purpose, and don't let anyone or anything distract you from your purpose.

For the resources that go with this and other chapters, including audio recordings and quick-reference cards, go to http://powerdiversity.com/the-library

Chapter 7: Practicing your skills

So you have taken the whole course. How does it feel to know the answers to questions that few people know, and fewer even bother to ask? Pretty good, huh?

Now it's time to implement your skills, and strengthen your Slayer muscles. I hope you have learned that being a Slayer is more about you than about the EVs you encounter, and that slaying Energy Vampires is more about transformation than elimination. Becoming a Slayer is about YOU.

Remember: The journey to becoming a Slayer is a long and difficult one, but if it were easy, everyone would be on it. It will take practice, and dedication, but if you are committed, and you must be to have gotten this far, you will succeed, as have the Slayers who have gone before you.

That said, now that you are ready to declare to the world that you are a Slayer, remember that more EVs than ever will start to seek you out, and test your skills. This is a good thing. Remember that difficult people are simply master teachers, here to show us where we are in our development. Welcome them and bless them, and in turn, you will be blessing yourself.

Homework:

- Print out the Energy Vampire Slayer ID card in the back of this book, along with a small picture of yourself to place in it, and have the card laminated. You can do this at any copy center, such as Copy Max or Kinko's.
- Review your Personal Compass every morning for 30 days.
- For the next 30 days, choose one Slayer principle every day (again, you'll find a list in the back of this book), and focus on that principle throughout the day.
- Choose a new quick reference every week, and keep that card around where you can see it--maybe on your desk, or on the wall, and practice until you have mastered the technique.
- Stop by http://www.powerdiversity.com and ask us questions in the HELP ME DAN section, and participate in the blog; ask questions and tell your stories of EV encounters.
- Never stop learning and developing. Contact us at learn@powerdiversity.com if you need any help or suggestions.
- Listen to at least one podcast per week at http://www.powerdiversity.com/podcasts. Let the world know that you are now a Slayer. Post it on your Facebook page, your blog, Tweet it, print it, email it, and never stop

proclaiming that you will combat and defeat Energy Vampires, Negaddicteds, and toxic attitudes wherever you encounter them.

🌑**Always remember that the goal is not just elimination of toxicity. The goal is transformation. If you truly transform yourself, you will also transform the world around you.**

This is the point where I must leave you to fly on your own, but like any good teacher, I will never abandon you. If you need anything, any time, contact me at dan@powerdiversity.com, and I will see a Slayer symbol appear in the sky wherever I am, and I'll be there to help.

This will conclude your first course in Energy Vampire Slaying.

Good luck. ***Until our next lesson...***

For the resources that go with this and other chapters, including audio recordings and quick-reference cards, go to http://powerdiversity.com/the-library

ENERGY VAMPIRE SLAYING: 101

QUICK-REFERENCE FLASH-CARDS

MY PERSONAL COMPASS

I AM:

_____
_____
_____

I'M HERE TO:

_____
_____
_____

I WANT:

_____
_____
_____

I WILL:

_____
_____
_____

1

4 Magic Phrases to Get You Out of Any Communication Jam:

1) That's interesting; tell me more.
2) That's interesting: why would you say that?
3) That's interesting; why would you do that?
4) That's interesting; why would you ask that?

Remember to listen to the audio that goes with the above tactic at:

http://powerdiversity.com/podcasts

2

THE PLATINUM RULE:

TREAT
OTHERS
THE
WAY

THEY

WANT
TO
BE
TREATED.

3

2 COMPONENTS OF A COPING STATEMENT:

1- They are positively phrased.
2- They are in the present.

4

HEMISPHERE SWITCHING 101

1-Lift your chin up

2-Recite your phone number backwards including the area code.

DANGER	POWER
Calm down	I understand...
I understand how...	I understand why...
No offense, but...	delete phrase
Don't take this the the wrong way, but...	delete phrase
I need/you need...	Place the powerful subject first
I'm sorry	I apologize
The "F" word (used to refer to gay people)	Words of Death
The "N" word (used to refer to black people)	Words of Death

MY COPING STATEMENTS:

_____

_____

_____

_____

_____

THE EXPLODER

1. POSITION YOURSELF
2. VALIDATE
3. COMPLIMENT
4. AGREE
5. TRANSITION WITH PERMISSION

POWER PHRASES:
"Oh that's horrible."
"You're in Luck."
"You've found the right person!"
"I can see you're upset"
"You're right!"
"If you can just give me a chance…"

DANGER PHRASES:
"Calm down."
"You need..."
"I understand how you feel."

THE CRY-BABY

1. HAVE YOUR TOOLS AT HAND
   1. BOX OF TISSUE
   2. BOTTLE OF WATER
2. DO NOT MAKE PHYSICAL CONTACT
3. FRONT-TILT AND WIDE-EYES
4. ASK CLOSED-ENDED QUESTIONS
5. MAKE THE OFFERING
6. USE THE BROKEN RECORD

POWER PHRASES
"Do you need a minute or two to compose yourself?"
"Are you ready now?"
"I can see you're upset, however..."

DANGER PHRASES
"What's wrong?"
"Don't cry."
"Why are you so upset?"
"Tell me about...(anything)"
"Oh, that's horrible..."

9

THE GOSSIP
Give them an **I-C-R**:
I-introduced
C-criticized
R-revealed

Here's how it sounds: "Mary, you just **introduced** Lawanda into our conversation, **criticized** her personally, and **revealed** some pretty sensitive information about her to me. *Was that your intent*?

POWER PHRASES
"I am only comfortable talking about people who are present."
"Would you like to go get Lawanda, or shall I?"

DANGER PHRASES
"Why don't you just shut up?"
"You're such a Gossip."
"Tell me more."
"I'm going to tell Lawanda you said that."

10

THE NEGADDICTED

1. LAY THE GROUNDWORK
2. SHOOT POWER PHRASES
3. SUGGEST ALTERNATIVE VIEWPOINTS
4. ASK THEM QUESTIONS
5. RUN AS FAST AS YOU CAN

POWER PHRASES
"I'm really trying to keep things positive--it's for my health--can you help me do that, please?"
"What do you think would make it better?"
"Watch--you'll love it" (coupled with the broken record).
"Maybe you should talk to someone about that."

DANGER PHRASES
"I agree." (When you really don't...)
"Is there anything I can do?"
"You're right."
"You're so negative."

11

THE SNIPER

1. GET INTO POSITION
2. CALL THEM BY NAME
3. BACKTRACK
4. ASK A SPOTLIGHT QUESTION

POWER PHRASES
"Are you trying to..."
"Why would you say that?"
"Why would you ask that?"
"Ooh, that hurt."
"I don't communicate like that, and I'd appreciate it if you didn't communicate like that with me."

DANGER PHRASES
"You're an idiot."
"That's not nice."
"Oh yeah, well..."
"I don't appreciate..."

12

THE TIME-SUCKER

1. MAKE AN AVAILABILITY MONITOR
2. SCRIPT OUT A TALK
3. USE YOUR AVAILABILITY MONITOR

POWER PHRASES
""I'm really trying to stay focused and stop getting distracted when I'm at work."
"If you could help me by checking my Availability Monitor..."
"I am right in the middle of something...can you shoot me an email and I'll get back to you?"

DANGER PHRASES
"Leave me alone"
"Can't you see I'm busy?"
"I just have a minute"
"Can it wait?"
"WHAAAAAT?"

13

THE TANK

1. INTERRUPT THEM
2. AGREE WITH THEM
3. GIVE THEM BOTTOM-LINE STATEMENTS
4. GIVE THEM BOUNDARY STATEMENTS
5. USE A RE-DIRECT WITH ASSUMPTIONS
6. USE EMPOWERMENT STATEMENTS

POWER PHRASES
"Bill! Bill Bill!" (Or whatever his/her name is)
"You're right!"
"I don't allow..."
"I do want to hear everything you have to say, but not in this manner."
"When you're ready to...I'll be ready to..."

DANGER PHRASES
"Excuse me...if I could just say something..."
"Would you please settle down?"
"If you would just listen..."
"You're just plain wrong."
"I'm not going to stand here and listen to this."

14

THE BEGGAR

1 – SYMPATHIZE
2 – SAY *NO*
3 – SAY WHY
4 – SUGGEST ALTERNATIVES
5 – USE THE BROKEN RECORD

POWER PHRASES
"Under Normal Circumstances..."
"Unfortunately I can't"
"I have other plans."
"It's not in my budget."
"I simply can't."
"Because, I just can't."

DANGER PHRASES
"I'm sorry."
"I understand how you feel."
"I'd like to."
"Let me think about it."
"No."

15

THE VICTIM

1. GIVE THEM A DESC SCRIPT
2. GIVE AN EXAMPLE
3. USE THE THREE-STEP "DITCHING" TECHNIQUE
   1. USE A "STOP" GESTURE
   2. USE THE VICTIM'S NAME
   3. MAKE YOUR EXIT

POWER PHRASES
"I'm glad you're not dwelling on it."
"Thanks for reminding me--I'm going to go write in my Gratitude Journal."
"You should talk to someone about that."
"Now that you know, you can break that cycle, huh?"

DANGER PHRASES
"Oh, come on--is it really that bad?"
"Oh, that's horrible."
"Do you want to talk about it?"
"How can I help?"

16

THE BULLY

PHYSICALLY:
1. STAND UP STRAIGHT
2. MAKE DIRECT EYE CONTACT
3. DON'T CROSS YOUR ARMS
4. LEAN IN WITH YOUR CHEST OUT
5. TILT YOUR HEAD FORWARD
6. USE THE THREE-SECOND LOOK

VERBALLY:
7. USE THEIR FIRST NAME
8. USE A SPOTLIGHT QUESTION
9. USE BOTTOM-LINE STATEMENTS
10. STAY ON MESSAGE W/ THE BROKEN RECORD

POWER PHRASES
"I don't respond to things like that."
"I don't communicate that way."

DANGER PHRASES
"I'm sorry..."
"What's wrong with you?"

17

HOW TO CRITICIZE WITH COMPLIMENTS

"You're too good at what you do to let things like this bring you down."

"You do so much already; you don't need additional problems like this to worry about."

"You're too well-respected to let something like this tarnish your professional reputation."

"I think so much of you, I felt I could be straight with you."

"You're too accomplished to let something like a simple personality conflict distract you from achieving your next goal."

18

THE FEEL-FELT-FOUND

1) Validate
2) Generalize
3) Respond

For example:

A customer says to you, "This is more of a hassle than what I was doing before!"

You could say, " I can understand why you would feel that some aspects of this are frustrating and inefficient. I have helped other customers who felt that way too when I first started working with them. However, after working with me to resolve the initial glitches, they found that this new process is not only more efficient, but more cost-effective too, and if you can just give me a chance, my name's Dan, and I know I can help you too. Would you give me a chance?"

19

Delivering a tricky message?

Try the PASSIVE VOICE instead of the ACTIVE VOICE

AV- It appears as though you didn't get your paperwork in on time.
PV- It appears as though the paperwork wasn't delivered on time.

_____

AV- You made a mistake.
PV- A mistake was made.

_____

AV- You need to send in your contract by Friday.
PV- The paperwork needs to be sent by Friday Morning.

20

ENERGY VAMPIRE SLAYING: 101

SLAYER PRINCIPLES

SLAYER PRINCIPLES

Light casts out darkness.

WWW.POWERDIVERSITY.COM

Energy Vampires hate the light and can't live in it.

WWW.POWERDIVERSITY.COM

What Energy Vampires say and do is about *them*, and a reflection of *them*.

WWW.POWERDIVERSITY.COM

What you say and do is about *you* and a reflection of *you*.

WWW.POWERDIVERSITY.COM

Every Slayer needs a few good magic power phrases.

WWW.POWERDIVERSITY.COM

A Slayer is in the *response* mode, as opposed to the *reaction* mode.

WWW.POWERDIVERSITY.COM

Out of control emotions make sane people crazy, and smart people stupid.

WWW.POWERDIVERSITY.COM

Every person you meet from now on is your *assignment*.

WWW.POWERDIVERSITY.COM

What's true on *any* level is true on *every* level.

WWW.POWERDIVERSITY.COM

Words are the most powerful things that exist. They are what create and destroy.

WWW.POWERDIVERSITY.COM

This page is designed to be printed out on standard 8x11 business-card paper.

SLAYER PRINCIPLES

Whatever effect your words
have on others, they will have
the exact same effect on you.

If you have the right words you
can do *anything*.

Slayers keep danger phrase and
power phrase lists.

You are in charge of every
relationship in your life.

You must do different *things* to
get different *results*.

Stay on message.

What gets *rewarded* gets
repeated.

Slayers don't use
words of death.

EVs expect a certain result from
their behavior--give them
something other than what
they're expecting, and it throws
them off course.

People treat you the way you
allow them to treat you.

This page is designed to be printed out on standard 8x11 business-card paper.

SLAYER PRINCIPLES

We *train* people how to treat us.

Those who gossip *with* you gossip *about* you.

You can't shine bright light without charging your own batteries. Feed your body, mind, and spirit with things that nourish them.

In your defenselessness your safety lies.

It is not our job to teach Energy Vampires a lesson; it is *their* job to teach *us* a lesson.

Hurting People Hurt People.

The Slayer asks not to win the war, but to be raised above the battlefield.

It is an impossibility that people will treat me better than I treat myself.

You must say *yes* to yourself before you can say *no* to others.

I can choose to be *kind* rather than to be *right*.

This page is designed to be printed out on standard 8x11 business-card paper.

SLAYER PRINCIPLES

If EVs knew how to show us
their greatness while getting
their needs met *they would*.

I am my brother's keeper.

You are always either spreading
light, or spreading darkness.
Even if just for today, focus on
spreading light.

Today is about me.
Every experience I have is
about me. It's all about me.

Difficult people and EVs appear
to show us who *we* are.

In this moment, I am either
conforming, or transforming--
the choice is mine.

I am here to show the world
what greatness looks like.

I am kind out of self-interest.

Never let *facts* get in the way of
the *truth*.

Energy Vampire Slaying is all
about me, not about the EVs.

This page is designed to be printed out on standard 8x11 business-card paper.

SLAYER PRINCIPLES

The question is not what to *do*;
the question is who to *be*.

*Every moment of every day you
are making a choice that will
bring you either closer to, or
farther away from, your destiny.*

Every person you meet from
now on is your assignment.

*Your gift is your curse and your
curse is your gift.*

*A Slayer has something to write
with and something to write on
at all times-- always always
always. No exceptions.*

How you do anything is how
you do everything.

How you treat anyone is how
you treat everyone.

Time is the coin of my life, and I
will choose how to spend it.

The better someone feels while
around you, the more power
you *both* have.

What you invest in shows, and
what you focus on grows.

This page is designed to be printed out on standard 8x11 business-card paper.

ABOUT THE AUTHOR

Communication expert Dan O'Connor has been helping individuals and organizations develop their communication and critical thinking skills for over fifteen years. Recognized both nationally and internationally, Dan came to prominence through his development and delivery of programs that include dealing with difficult and demanding people, understanding and dealing with different personality types, speaking with power and precision, professional communication and etiquette, developing your personal compass, transformational thinking, customer service scripts and techniques, team-building and many many more—all programs based on self-development and powerful communication.

Having witnessed the business problems caused by office energy vampires, workplace negativity, interpersonal conflicts, and employees and supervisors struggling to "find the words," Dan began developing tactical training programs that go beyond theory, and focus on scripts, phrases, communication systems, and memory techniques designed to deliver instant results.

The instant results? Transformation--both personal and professional.

Dan has produced countless personal and professional communication training resources, including top-rated blogs, seminars, articles, and more. His latest works include Communicate in America (professional communication training program), Energy Vampire Slaying:101 (dealing with difficult people program), and his number-one rated podcast, Professional Communication Tactics.

Dan travels out of Fargo, ND, USA, and can be reached at dan@powerdiversity.com.

Look for Say This--NOT THAT!!

Made in the USA
Las Vegas, NV
29 November 2022

60645104R00063